The Collected Poems of
Geoffrey Holloway

Edited and Introduced by David Morley

ARROWHEAD
PRESS

First published 2007 by
Arrowhead Press

70 Clifton Road, Darlington
Co. Durham, DL1 5DX
Tel: (01325) 260741

Typeset in 11pt Laurentian by
Arrowhead Press

Email: editor@arrowheadpress.co.uk
Website: http://www.arrowheadpress.co.uk

© *The estate of Geoffrey Holloway 2007*

ISBN: 978-1-904852-16-2

All rights reserved. No part of this book may be reproduced, stored in a retrieval system, or transmitted in any form, or by any means, electronic, mechanical, photocopying, recording or otherwise, without prior written permission from the author's eatate or Arrowhead Press.

Requests to publish works from this book should be sent to Arrowhead Press.

The author's rights have been asserted under Section 77 of the Copyright, Designs and Patents Act 1988

Arrowhead Press acknowledges the financial assistance of Arts Council England North East.

Arrowhead Press is a member of Independent Northern Publishers.

Printed by Athenaeum Press, Gateshead, Tyne and Wear.

The Author

CONTENTS

Frontispiece Portrait of the author	ii
INTRODUCTION	xvi
ACKNOWLEDGEMENTS	xix

TO HAVE EYES (1972)
Double Vision: Spring	1
Going to School	2
Doing the Length	2
Head of a Friend	3
Dead Boy	3
The Shot Dove	4
Going for a Song	4
Hunger	5
Fat Woman	5
Hope	6
Village	7
Haiku for the Return of a Goddess	7
Haiku: In the Bay	8
Twelve Senryu	9
Troubadour	10
Twister	10
Painter's Country	11
Baroque	12
Missionary	12
To a Calf Born on Sunday, in a Field	13
Spring She Says	13
Thaw	14
Samadhi	15

RHINE JUMP (1974)
Rhine Jump	19
Five Parachutists	20
Ballad of the Seagone Scouse	23
Ode to the River Severn	24
Act of God	26

At a Checkpoint	27
Peace With Hunger	28
Summer Storm	28
History: A Butcher's Hook	29
Rain Before Dawn	29
Nature Notes	30
Stock	31
Forewarned	32
The Recidivists	33
On Clem: A Cat	34
Neighbours	35
Surd	35
Venus	35
Toad Tracks	35
Galatea	37
One Up on Circe	38
Woman of the Philistines	39
Placings	41
Command Performance	42
Summer School	42
Gladiolus	43
Free Skating Champion	44
Prospecting the Reserves	45
Tenure	46

ALL I CAN SAY (1975)
1 Mouths, Words

Answering the Child	47
End of a Cat	47
No More	48
Snails	48
Slugs	49
Snail Thrush	49
Woodpecker	50
Blooded	50
Ewe	51
Totem Animal	53
Enigma	53
Rebuke	54
Caged	54
Shore Pickings	55

2 *The Truth Of It*

Lament for Prophets	57
For Vernon Watkins, Cum Grano Salis	57
The Vandals	58
Messiah	59
Jesting Pilate	59
No Brassards, You'll Give the Battalion away	60
Proof	60
Siblings	61
One for the Lord	61
Soft Mick	61
Initiation	62
Heirlooms	63
Obituaries	63
Operation Usurper	64
Martyr	64
Night Call	65
Waking	65
Village Church: Capo di Sorrento	65
Village Cemetery	66
Geranium Summer	66
July Field	67
The Optics of Holism	68
Street	68
Definitive	69
Two Riddles and a Proverb	70

3 *A Latrine In Purgatory*

Bedsitters	71
Three Star	72
Anachronism	72
Romantic	73
Foreshore	74
Lily of the Valley	74
Nasturtiums	75
Traveller's Joy	75
Bitch	77
The Children	78
Fidelity	78
Statistics: 2 a.m.	79
Non-Accidental Injury Slides	80

4   Tears On The Wind

Odalisque Extraordinary	81
BH	83
Dowser's Funeral	83
Widower	84
Highwayman	84
Irreparable	85
Surplus	85
Purpose Built	86
A Question of Time	86
Old Woman Blues	87
Old Man Blues	87
Antics	88
Surveillance	88
Supper	90

THE CRONES OF APHRODITE (1985)

1   The Golden Bucket

True North	91
Sex Kitten	91
The Lovers	92
Foreplay	93
Independence Day	93
Gynae Ward	94
Leapfrog	95
Brushoff	95
Canine Interlude	96
Eye Of The Iguana	97
Stopover Junction	97
Macho	98
Jacob At Fifty	98

2   Smells Like A War

Never Such A Game	100
For My Father	101
For My Father (2)	102
Song Of An Airborne Widow	103
Home Of The Brave	104
Semblance	104
To A Wartime Pro	105
Standing Orders: Hamburg	106
Fun Beach	107

3   The Slow Conveyor Belt

Sunday Canal	108
Shropshire Union	108
Ludlow Castle	109
Trafalgar Square	110
Waterloo Bridge	110
From Castleton Through The Winnatts	111
High Wire	112
Brands Hatch Widow	113
Tides	113

4   Bury Me Anywhere

Passion Flower	114
Gale	114
Lawn Mowing	115
Sweet Peas	115
The Virtue Of Slovenliness	116
Drought	117
A Chrysanthemum Named Cardinal	117
Grass	118
Jardin Sous La Pluie	118
Rain	119

SALT, ROSES, VINEGAR (1986)

Frontiers	121
Scapegoat	122
Springboard	122
Things	123
Epicentres	123
A Timely Surgery	124
Son	125
No Answer	126
In the Pines	126
Salt, Roses, Vinegar	127
Cain	127
Death of a Gambler	128

PERCEPTS WITHOUT DEFERENCE (1987)

Author's Note on Welsh Forms	129
Twenty Englynion	129
Lament	133
Poet	134
Sleep Charm	135
Gnomic Stanzas	135
Garden Cywydd	136
Llatai Poem	136

MY GHOST IN YOUR EYE (1988)

Threnody	137
Scorpion	139
The Abominable Snowman	140
Landslip Terrace	141
Interviewing the Megaboss	142
Bow Street Rag	143
Night Birds: Newcastle	144
Mill Hands: Colden Valley	145
Autumn Salient	146
Kin	147
So This Is Where You Are	148
Arthritic	149
Shangri La	150
Stillborn Dialogue	151
Therapeutic Abortion	152
Flesh As Grass	154
Jeux D'Enfants	155
Virtuoso	156
Bowls	156
Fixtures	157
Something Else	158
Eden	159
The Sign	159
Paying Back	160
Poems For Hope	161
Inconsumable	162
Psychokinesis	163
Options	164
Only Too True Story	165

THE STRANGEST THING (1991)

The Strangest Thing	167
Getting It Straight	168
Severn Minnows	169
Refugees: Belgium 1940	170
Border Ballad	171
History Lesson	171
Catatonic	172
The Glass People	173
It	173
Armada	174
Parting	175
Divorce	175
Sweets of Eros	175
Genitals	176
Stepdaughter	177
With Students	178
Teenager	179
Executors	180
Get The Early Worm	181
Term Time	181
Slipway	182

MONGOOSE ON HIS SHOULDER (1992)

Godson	185
The Balloon	186
A Seat In Arcady	187
New Brighton Ferry	188
Cunarders	189
Hopes	189
Indian Rope Trick	191
Geordie Starlings	191
Here And Hereafter	192
South Pier: Blackpool	193
Tarn Birds	194
Blackbird	194
Thrush	195
Haiku	195
Church Bric-A-Brac	196
Kite Mondo	197
Male Sea Horse	198

It Was	199
Victims	200
Gone	201
Window Seat	202
Veteran	202
Sea Horse	204
You	204
Oedipus at Newmarket	205
From the Chinese	205
Village	206
Wet Day	206
Dialogue In The Small Hours	207

THE LEAPING POOL (1993)

Trade	209
Taken	210
Gone To Sea	210
Estuary	211
Ann's Lullaby	211
Fancy Woman	212
Survivor	212
Graffiti	213
Last Resort	213
Riviera	214
Boardsailor	214
Tube Travellers	215
Dipper	215
Tenement	216
Swiss Cottage	217
Rainforest Child	218
Park Familiar	219
Churchyard Stroll	220
Mainstreet Hotel	221
Dear	222
Comedian	223
The Price	223
Lisa	224
Between Sea And Grass	224
Here	225
Swot	225
Diesel Driver	226

Clearing The Attic	228
Drunk	228
The Gaffers	229
Senior Citizen	230
Stroke	230
Monitors	232
An Essay On The Shaking Palsy	233
Blind Date	234
Cross My Heart	235
Salt 'N Vinegar	236
Still Life	238

A SHEAF OF FLOWERS (1994)

Alder	239
Allotments: February	239
April Dusk	240
Anti-Nuclear Demo	240
Atishoo Atishoo	241
Aubade	242
Family Funeral	243
Bathroom Flies	244
Beach-Head	245
Dear Second Bed Down	245
Comeback	246
A Sheaf Of Flowers	247
Old Man	248
Penultimate	249
Progress	250
The Elect	250
Fireworks On The Rec	252
Long Meg And Her Daughters	253
Last Days	254
Lazarus	255
A Proper Woman	255
Diet	256
Inmates	257
Generations	258
Gig	258
House Arrest	259
Roe Deer: Sunset	260
October	260

Snow On Grub Street	261
Takeover	261
Tramp Steamers	262
Travelling Man	262
Vacant Possession	263
Where Fish Are, God Is	264
Vegetarian's Vertigo	265
When I'm Seventeen	266

AND WHY NOT? (1997)

Night People	267
Ballad of the Axe	268
The Assignment	269
A Look at the 'D' Word	271
Birthday Greetings to Myself at Seventy-Four	272
Flesh	273
Satirist	273
Bedside Manners	274
Blue Films	275
Early, Late	275
Cenotaph	276
That Thing	277
River Bank	277

UNCOLLECTED POEMS

Dusk	279
World War Two Calendar:	
Shakespeare Day	280
Sherlock Holmes Day	280
Good Friday	280
Saint Patrick's Day	281
V E Day	281
Old Thoughts Walking on a Fine Night	282
The Legacy	282
Tenses	283
A Late Gift	284
Time Share	284
Bench-Marks	285
After Rain	285
Hero	286

Snow Folk	287
Father William is Somewhat Exercised	288
As if it Mattered	290
The Genetics of Snow	291
Migrant	292

INTRODUCTION

David Morley

Geoffrey Holloway was born in Birmingham in 1918. His early years were spent between Liverpool and Shrewsbury. Before the war he worked in the Shropshire County Library, then in 1939 he went into the Royal Army Medical Corps, serving in a field ambulance, a general hospital and, later, in 225 Para Field Ambulance, dropping on D-Day and over the Rhine. After the war he went to Southampton University, emerging with a qualification in Social Science. He then worked in a mental hospital, as a Prisoner's Aid Society agent, and from 1953 to his retirement in 1983 as a mental health worker for Westmorland then Cumbria County Council, where he lived in the same village, Staveley, for over forty years. He was one of the leading spirits of the group called the Cumbrian Poets that included, among others – William Scammell, Christopher Pilling, David Scott, Jacob Polley, Neil Curry, Patricia Pogson, Peter Rafferty, M.R. Peacocke and Norman Nicholson.

However, Holloway was not some local poetic hero. He began to publish poems nationally as early as 1946, contributing to the *Times Literary Supplement, The Listener, Encounter, London Magazine, Yorkshire Post, PN Review, Poetry Review* and countless other small magazines and anthologies. He was also an intensely active and visible figure in the small press scene for many decades. In some ways you could say that he embodied that scene – moving between the mainstream and avant-garde with dexterity; developing a mastery of formal and free verse, of demotic as well as a classical syntax; and oscillating between the sublime and realism in subject and theme. What was always consistently right in his work was tone. This was all his own, and his integrity of feeling and response was the heart of it. His many subjects included the memory of war, the consolation and difficulty of love, and his alert responses to the natural world. With W.S. Graham, his exact contemporary, he was one of the most distinctive voices in twentieth century British poetry, with a genuinely gifted ear for the music and the movement of language.

Readers recognised and responded to his gifts. Between 1972 and 1997 Holloway published twelve collections of poetry, including the book that established his reputation, *Rhine Jump*, a Poetry Book Society Choice in 1974. *Rhine Jump* is an astonishing book which still yields a huge energy and alertness in its language. Subject-wise, it feels like a massive gamble made by a poet who did not wish to speak much about his war experience, but could no longer resist the ghosts trying to speak through him. The honesty and humility in its tone makes the book very distinctive and necessary within our own time. It is still one of the best places to start reading him.

Geoffrey Holloway died in October 1997. He was mourned by his many friends and admirers, by fellow poets and dedicated readers – his books were cherished by those who possessed them. Holloway's reputation as a poet quietly increased as more and more readers and writers began to realise not only how much they missed his presence, but how much they missed the poems that made a small magazine worth reading because it had Geof's poems in it. After his death, Holloway's poetry also became important to some poet-critics. He occupied a similar critical position to W.S. Graham. That is, his excellence was in danger of oblivion through simple neglect. Like Graham, Holloway needed critical champions. Not only that, but many readers also voiced the necessity for a *Collected Poems*, for Holloway's work to be offered to generations of new readers.

Therefore, when Geoffrey Holloway's widow, the poet Patricia Pogson, contacted me with a view to editing his work, I could not have been more honoured. Geof had been exceptionally kind to me when I was making my way as a young poet and scientist, looking at my early poems and suggesting reading. To my mind, he was, and remains, a poetic exemplar. What I then set myself to do is read, digitise, and then check every poem from every volume published by the poet during his lifetime. These included more easily available volumes such as *All I Can Say* from Anvil Press (1978), but also cyclostyled and stapled pamphlets with short print-runs such as *Percepts Without Deference* – Holloway's bold attempt to write contemporary English-language poetry within strict Welsh verse forms – from the fugitive press Aquila (1987). Patricia also photocopied poems that had appeared in magazines but were unpublished in volume form, and sent these along to me for consideration and scanning. She forwarded other poems she considered substantial – including the delightful 'Migrant' dedicated to his friend the poet Gerda Mayer which features as the final poem in this book.

In some ways, the easiest part of the project was over once the book was edited – for publishing a *Collected Poems* is itself a greater feat these days than putting the poems together. Before his death, Holloway had complained to me about the problems and pitfalls of poetry publishing in the United Kingdom. The haphazard nature of the enterprise had caused him to migrate from press to press. He knew also that, although that poetry publishing had its difficulties, when you made that leap into publication, getting the British poetry world to give notice to the output of any small, independent press was nigh-impossible. Faber, Chatto,

Secker and Oxford University Press were the sleekly visible part of a small but skewed market in the 1970s and 1980s, and there was worse to come.

By the mid to late 1990s, if poetry were a species, it would have entered the red list. Bigger publishers dropped their poetry lists or shrank them to a trickle of slim, overpriced volumes. Prominent poets, once published by the big houses, were forced to seek out new habitats within powerful specialist presses such as Carcanet and Bloodaxe. However, one of the unpredicted and unpredictable results of this cultural shockwave was the subsequent *rise* of independent small publishers, and an increasing sophistication in their publishing and marketing methods – not least through the use of websites and print-on-demand technology. New presses such as Arrowhead Press, Salt and Heaventree began to occupy some of the ground left by mainstream operators, and show them not only how to do the job better but how to keep their stable of poets in print. I suspect that Geoffrey Holloway would have been wryly amused to know that his *Collected Poems* is now published entirely within a renewed – if still penniless – independent sector, and again by a specialist press in the North of England.

When I was scanning his poems into my computer, a letter to me from Geof fell out of one of the books. In that letter he voiced his desire for more pleasure and challenge in contemporary poetry. As he put it he wanted 'to hear poems by folk who speak personally, directly, lyrically if you like. One to one.' We no longer have the pleasure of Geof's company, or the delight of any new poems, but we do now have the pleasure of this book which contains all of the pieces he published. Personally, directly and lyrically, this book returns him to us, one to one.

DM, Warwick, March 2007.

ACKNOWLEDGEMENTS

Patricia Pogson was central to the making of this book. Neil Curry prompted the project, read the pre-final manuscript and made helpful comments. Roger Collett and Joanna Boulter at Arrowhead Press bravely took on this book.

My thanks are also due to all the individuals and organisations who have helped, especially colleagues in the Warwick Writing Programme and the Department of English and Comparative Literary Studies at the University of Warwick; to my wife Dr Siobhan Keenan with whom I discussed the poems and the various drafts of the book; and to Michael Schmidt for his encouragement with the project at a time when I thought it might not succeed.

Finally, we acknowledge all Geof's publishers for their generosity in allowing us to print these poems. Their names make for a roll call of great independent publishing. *Anvil Press. Aquila Pamphlet Poetry. Arc Publications* (on behalf of *Littlewood Press*). *Crabflower Pamphlets. Enitharmon Press* (on behalf of *London Magazine Editions*). *Flambard Press. Free Man's Press. Grand Piano Editions. National Poetry Foundation. Redbeck Press.*

To those saints of the small press, thank you.

Cover photograph:
Haweswater in Autumn   ©*Wayne Hutchinson/FLPA*

TO HAVE EYES

DOUBLE VISION: SPRING

The cat among the grasses nodding as it sniffs —
like a new-bathed infant shaping for a kiss.
The swans opulent, their bulrush-furry throats
ringed, rippling, with filamented light.
Shadows that are swallow-blue, yet brittle-clear,
that match the trespass of chrysanthemums released
by lancing heels of divers whanged from trees —
and all along the towpath the spun rod,
the dainty float cavorting in the sun.
To have eyes. To see.

The stagnant salmon like a crippled submarine
leprous in the shallows by the dripping arch —
a bone-white mouth insensitively working,
a quiet stammer, hung with sentences of death.
What was colour, kick and phallic exultation,
that shook the stream with the torpedoes of a myth,
laid-up like David for a chit of useless warmth,
like sunken David (that prodigious king)
for a stone tribute, a buck's delinquent sling.
To have eyes. To see.

GOING TO SCHOOL

'It's smashing early-on, clean and lonely!' Then:
'I like it with the car-wireless, music swishes
up and down the little hills!' Then:
'The waterweeds — green straw!' And:
'I don't look at the sun in prayers; it makes me sneeze!'

So she skips, babbles, imperious summer
frisking with her like a favourite pup,
says what she thinks without thinking, if it touched
her off that way assuredly would try
a handstand against the blue-walled sky . . .

while the water-doubled cherries dip
great spinnakers of bloom,
the haycarts of the willows trail
to harvest-homes of gold, and I,
returning that irradiant way,

find records of her breezy coming
constellated on the green:
magnolia-petals: butterflies
that broached a season's nectar-vats
to settle on its wavy grass sensuous profundities.

DOING THE LENGTH

After a month of scuffling with the testy wave
— her last attempt abruptly dashed
by the backwashed spray of some galvanic grampus
flailing blind seconds off a daily stint —
she makes her way to that disturbing deep-end,
to challenge failure, try again.

At a nodded word we're off, I
with an easy sidestroke looking back,
unsuccessfully trying to mask a grin
at such heroic painful dedication
— the gobstopper eyes, face bleached with effort,
below the tight red-rubber cap.

Doggedly she comes, Kotch my daughter,
with the gull-slanted nickname, the neat scooping
breaststroke (looking always, too quick to last) . . .
through the tossed shadow, the long stare
of the loosely-wadered tall attendant:
a propitious milestone mounted half-way.

For once in its welter that channel's clear —
amazingly she nears, touches, then
collapses into my slippery arms —
weak with triumph, round my body-pole
like some royal flag after its wide climax,
suddenly nerveless, wind-limp.

We towel, dress, saunter home talking . . .
how at last she's pipped her schoolmate, soon
will manage half-miles without a change of breath.
Already she's a mite disinterested,
dreaming up some newer, kinkier sport,
growing out of, passing on . . .

Thirty yards. A trivial garland,
in a stretched rainwater butt, and yet
something I've done, that she has now —
that both allow, of which both are proud
differently, yet mutually owned —
covenantal, the tighter since unspoken.

And this, cardinal: a cord of grace
giving strange substance to the loined accident,
tying one into acute paternity,
baptizing in the name of father, love.
Thirty yards, learning to swim, be . . .
within the pooled corroborated heart.

HEAD OF A FRIEND

Unremarkable at first; that is, until
the magnetism's realised.
Then, attempting it in profile seems
gratuitous, impossible.

The cut, square; the nose less
some copyright of cold Athene
than the beak of an ironic sparrow-hawk;
curved tautly, out of Dürer or Bellini.

The mouth straight; the chin, convinced;
antiphonal, with the rest so placed
one stress deflected would precipitate
a cadence glaring as a mutilation.

Above all, eyelids: their level gleam
through the fronds, say, of some half-Delphic cigarette . . .
And what's beneath no longer questioned, left
securely to reflect its fame:

a clean sincerity so calmly lit,
so frankly effortless the colour seems
less grey than its incarnate distillation, —
so native, here, one doesn't notice it.

DEAD BOY

She could forgive the wind
its thievish importunity;
pummelling the roped bough
as if seconds only
held the favour of the fruit.

She could not forgive
the insult of its tenderness:
its casual, brotherly remembrance;
pushing idly, too-visibly,
a half-grown ghost upon a swing.

THE SHOT DOVE

'Transmute your grief into aesthetic gain.'
One's own, perhaps. But can the phrase refine
impersonally some one else's pain?

Not simple, surely, with an epithet
to sponge away the fever-sweat,
leaving sorrow cool and happy in its debt.

Behind the art-harmony, the spectral prism
of sun-shot elegy and euphemism
moves the smashed original, the pitiless swift spasm, —

while away from rhetoric, the proud tact
of the flowered catafalque silken-tricked,
the Word must bow to its abandoned fact:

the rigid wedge of cancer jamming the breast's love,
the rifled air despairing after the shot dove,
feathers in the furtive snow, bright-tinged above.

GOING FOR A SONG

Nothing too recherché this afternoon.
The skull, Tenth Ideology.
Typically dictatorial (note the jaw).
But died oddly; natural causes it would seem.

Next, a torso, nigger-brown;
strategically preserved in jazz, alcohol.
Could have been a plantation ornament.
Not rare; especially in some places.

Third (one of a pair) a female breast, —
for passround later if desired.
Notched. I would suggest
a nursing mother's, distributed at feed.

Last, a child's foot.
Gaudy, perhaps.
But with the maker's mark in genuine napalm.
Unpriced. Modern, at a guess.

HUNGER

Because of me, the hawk's telescopic
patience in the poised sky.

Because of me, the child's ballooning
belly, vestigial eye . . .

the jagged knuckles, scrawled indecent
banners, contumacious feet;

undercover carnage
of tapeworm, spirochaete.

Because of me, the fanclubbed scream
of the teenager loin-dry;

the creviced inconclusive oddments —
lipsticked parson, stained boy.

Because of me, the black heat,
embrace of terror, fanged retreat;

because I'm eaten, eat.

FAT WOMAN

She is many. Basements and gossips know her,
the doctor (when he has to), the undertaker.

Sometimes (for economy) silent, in the dark;
monstrous with herself, a stringless 'cello.

At others, plaintive, hostile: either
candle-greasy, in a huddle of self-pity,

or frantic, flouncing at the rent-man,
her lower lip shoved out like a dead slug.

Humour could have oiled the creases for her;
instead, anxiety's a jealous clock:

each jackboot minute tramps, tramps . . .
till belongings shiver, the walls quake.

Or there's strangling fear (of rape, rebellion,
her own stuffed insufferable desires). . .

then, every minute insulted she hoards, swells
with perfect rancour, infinite compensation.

Is there a stray kitten to commandeer,
that she daren't let out to mess, even . . .

hope's toy (buttered, bullied)
its claws pretty, only skin-deep?

No matter. Ancestrally betrayed,
in a blubbery rut, a crooked gland-pattern,

she must live out her terrifying muchness;
and gone, suffer a bony verdict:

'Wouldn't stint the appetite. Heart, you know.'

HOPE

You build. The bleary cobweb
demoralises art.
Damp drags the ceiling, squats
like thunder on the heart.

You marry. Irrespective,
toppling in the sun,
like syrup off a knife her golden
senses writhe and run.

Is your sister's name a trumpet
declamatory, strong?
A little twisted finger
sells you for a song.

Is your brother a disciple?
Spying for the Board
he crows your ghostly assets
irredeemably abroad.

Time to hack a headstone,
relegate the lot.
'Here lies Hope the mason . . .
What never was, is not'.

VILLAGE

Let no one sentimentalise the view.
Eyes, a common grey,
like the brief skies they ruminate can stray
in a second, expressly glance
from sun-poised and prodigal
to stone-churlish, mist-sly.

Trust no-one longer than it takes. Wink
as they do, say the guarded eyes.
Hot, cold, within the forge of living
breeds a safe temper: rapier-shrewd
but with enough play to make an artful peace —
say the eyes, the restless eyes.

HAIKU FOR THE RETURN OF A GODDESS

Paphos. Its node, you, —
playing collective marbles.
Truly, flesh is hard.

Absent, your breasts have
me sleepless, water-lilies
pressing on a thought.

And the mouth's wanton,
its oppressive fantasies
a satyr's tonguing . . .

till there's rain-ransom,
the eyelids melt on a dream,
a choir of roses.

Then faith keel-cuts sleep,
the time's proud, impetuous,
rounding to its own.

A quay's expectant,
in the headlands of these arms
you're wave-won, homefast.

Apricot shadows.
Then the gulls' acclamation —
Venus, from the spray.

HAIKU: IN THE BAY

Sweaty, the shirt sticks.
The sky's larkspur and the clouds'
twisty thistledown.

Fawny grasshoppers,
telephoning each other
from adjacent stalks.

A slant of thunder.
The jets dividing heaven, —
white-rainbow-trailing.

The plated jetty.
A crocodile, basking. On
its snout men fishing.

By the roped lifebelt
boys kicking a landed crab,
their wanton fearful luck.

The prawns, holy-ghosting:
martyrs, their love transparent,
daring the sea's wound.

In a glassy calm
the yachts poised and scrupulous
as table napkins.

TWELVE SENRYU

Sodium lighting.
The near past, a valley of
incendiaries.

The bedfast cripple, —
an opaque geometry
sleepless with death-lust.

Salt in the marrow:
a hypochondriac told
he's looking better.

The rake fined for drink.
His name published. Worse, his age, —
that last false conquest.

A couple. Instead
of her having the baby
he carries the peke.

Her darling rabbit, —
an invalid, accomplished
for the sake of love.

The old gardener,
arthritis in his clubbed bones
a python, tensing.

Fire in the hotel.
The aesthetic chef, catching
its glow in a glass.

Gold and ruddy flesh
time-bitten, her account's face
a chasmed peachstone.

The wife's incessant
ultimatum. 'But for you,
I'd get a divorce!'

Erupted schoolkids,
pulling at parental years
like short-leashed puppies.

The flower-marquee.
Dismantled. Tickets, one for
a rose called 'Fortune'.

TROUBADOUR

Lady, take this my single heart, —
with it, one dormant coronary.
Have whichever chin you fancy (both at need),
my belly-wobble, each hairy nipple,
the knees arthritic with matted prayer . . .
eyes also, (provided they're released
for science when the rest's on tour).
Throw in a fungoid ear, two ripe carbuncles,
and — yours for the glorious resurrection —
one frost-nipped abashed rosebud —
plus soul to measure, if you're prone to such.
Take my all. Beloved, be
— for sweet Tithonus' sake —
my only true reliquary.
Take me for what 1 am, a pathologist's dream
of fair vermin, a knacker's yardstick.
Take me, take me.

You'd better. You're not so sharp yourself.

TWISTER

A change comes on, slow lefthand;
tonsured, creased with fat;
looking as if he hadn't puff
to roll never mind bowl it.

His new foursprung an oily leer,
first wicket down adjusts his grip:
feels day and crowd behind him, already
past deep mid-on the skimming zip.

Cruel to itself it lobs
— one dawdling astronomic tease —
huge as a beachball, begging for redress, —
hit me, hit me, please.

On the leg, too. Heaven-loosed.
Over the ropes man, write him off for ever.
A brave back-lift. Then the blade hisses, —
furious, flogs gaping air.

So's not to hurt too much only
one bail strokes off.
The keeper thuds experienced gloves.
Soft as patacake? Soft enough.'

PAINTER'S COUNTRY

Seurat might have managed this oatfield, now, —
punctilious as a feudal priest
accommodated each fawny seed-head:
kempt as a bead-frame, pointilliste.

Then the cypresses, green-twisty-baroque, —
pillars so vehement they'd scoff
at the sun-torpid villagers beneath . . .
palpably, Van Gogh.

What of that pheasant cometing the afternoon
— transfixing heaven with a rainbow lance —
who but Sutherland could have smelted-out,
felt, flushed, such royal resonance?

And here, in its foreground niche,
one white butterfly;
intimate Whistlerian suffix, —
so perfect it looks hardly dry.

BAROQUE

Ferns to start with:
curvy-backed and
long-headed, climbing out
of coiled shyness to parade
like sea-horses, fanciful.

Then bluebells, say:
each flowered stalk
a carillon of scrolled lanterns,
elegantly hung upon
the promise of a shepherd's crook.

Affected?
Pretty-pretty? Not
when mounted to illuminate
a witty sport of nature or
a saviour sitting up.

MISSIONARY

Like some old pedlar, doubled-up,
with a sack of firewood shoved
across his back,
down the path the young hedgehog
as if called expressly marches in.

We put him down a saucer, at the smell
his nostrils flicker wetly, he imbibes,
then with that tacky tread
cantilevered as before
is off again quite imperturbably.

Handled, he won't condense to spikes;
consistently declines to bunch
his fawn-black bristles; electing to remain
— as ever — the fearless innocent;
committed, indomitably sure.

Love he can't imagine, yet
— a prehistoric torchbearer —
occasions instinctively as breath;
kindling, like the tiny spills
his armoury suggests.

And, coming as it does, through front doors
and garden fences irrespectively,
his is the trim, the tough tenacious
oriflamme, that unreservedly must stray, —
and what it doesn't question, get.

TO A CALF BORN ON SUNDAY, IN A FIELD

Most tender, most topical of clowns,
so helpless, even, that I cannot laugh
at your gawkiness, the way you stumble, flop
from knobbly sticks to flounder frantically,
then dazed, half-kneeling, try once more
with stilted rear-legs furiously to force
the silly pair in front to hold
one noble second quite conclusively...
unforgettable, you that entered on the world
head-in-hooves, as if your sudden birth
were an interruption of some praying silence,
here, now, observe your triumph and beatitude.

Soon, a time must come
whose wit's too practical for simpletons like you,
too near the marrow for the unassuming funnybone.
Soon, it will be foot-rot, flies,
mists that suffocate, winds that drive
derisive, through the sodden, serf-marked ear..
Soon — perhaps indifferently — we'll watch
you passing anonymously by:
a roulette of eyeballs rolled without a chance
round the bars of a tumbril systematically trailing
to oblivion: a gun, a gaudy slab...

But this, this is your day.
Rest, therefore, in its sensuous immediacies,
tributes to the birthday of an innocence
no less the genuine if brittle, short.
Admit your charities: the lush lather
of a new coat with its poignant match
of early primrose, mushroom-grey;
the rough relish of a mother's tongue
painting, repainting, every fleck;
the grove of elders gazing
chestnut-eyed at these immense antics;
and the earth, the ancient pedestal,
straightening your feet, your novice knees;
setting you — this day at least — foursquare:
the fool-prince of an unbearable felicity,
heaven-schooled, among the buttercups.

SPRING SHE SAYS

Spring? (she says). A bit depressing at first,
beginning what one can't end:
all flighty blues and heady wind,
time zigzag, like a play of finches, —
capricious, too quick to hold.

Summer? A shapelier hammock; voluptuous, drowsy-rich, —
the looped honeysuckle nostril-high,
the butterflies spread like painted fans,
time in a drift of dandelion . . .
over grassroots, everything.

Autumn making its own sadness, all
banners and castles down:
thistles in a rearguard longing,
mauve pyres of woodsmoke through the dusk . . .
time a theme on a 'cello, vast, dying.

And Winter? The air crisp, cold, suddenly
bright-cold, so sharply peeled;
children in their new berets
like holly, local, everlasting;
and time kindness, maybe a true beginning.

THAW

Inbetween landscape: understated
fawn and sorrel surfacing;
the spectral stalks of last year grass,
residual leaves of this, —
with here, there, some scarlet windfall, —
rosehips, a robin's breast.

Look at the trees: their crammed buds
proleptic, pursed to give;
clear, for all that sackcloth sky.

No longer must the heron walk hungry,
on stunned water;
the stallion shiver its flesh out,
disconsolate, in starched hay.
Instead, peace smokes, unquenchable, from a kindled earth.

The blue roadway's runlet-scalloped;
melted into gleamy pools
the rigid hollows of the field.
Wheels singe, slither through.

Snow was deception: beneath that strict sheet
all the hard time love lay;
green with longing, awake now;
just a sleepy flake or so
still at the corners of her eyes.

SAMADHI

A wayside toad:
scummed and nubbly skin,
movelessness,
gold-rimmed gaze, —
reminding,

brusquely, of
the Delhi road,
and the sadhu, set
like a volcano
in his ash.

His trunk, harrowing:
a scarred scree;
the ends of him wrenched
like feudal wood
by chronic will, —

scrub, cut-back,
mere living, warped
into a darkening
topiary
of pride.

Yet to him, all
so much less
than nothing . . .
fossilry,
beginner's drill . . .

sitting his ages
by a Sun whose Word
long since
absolved all
vanity of eyes.

RHINE JUMP

RHINE JUMP, 1944

They dropped us on the guns, left us in a flaring
lurch of slipstream kicking like sprayed flies, —
till canopies shook sudden heads, inhaled, held
        a breath, —
alive again we slanted down,
too many, into their doomed sights,

On scrambled moment it was red, green,
dragging to the door of the Douglas then
falling through a monstrous aviary roof
on Guy Fawkes Night (only this was day)
into shrill scarifying glory…

then Germany, the Fatherland, a zooming field —
banged down on it, stood up among the chaos,
        with
fingers flopped like rubber gloves trying
to slap one's box, slough the afterbirth of chute,
make somehow that snatch of wood.

There were chutes already in those trees, caught:
battalion boys who'd dropped too late or
        drifted…
harness-ravelled, cocooned there —
like silkworms, moveless, wet…
so easy, against all that white.

But not so many resistive earthworms —
the early birds had seen to that.
Soon, it was rendezvous: a stodgy farm.
The war was folding: fight-thin.
Prisoners happened; columned, toneless.

Next day it was hearing tales again,
having a kip in a pigsty, scouting the dropping —
        zone
to get silk (knickers for sweethearts, wives);
maybe a green envelope, speculation
about leave, Japan.

Oh and a gun-pit by the way, an 88:
bodiless, nothing special, —
only the pro's interest in other's kit:
grey slacks for the use of, old, ersatz;
with a brown inside stripe: non-ersatz.

FIVE PARACHUTISTS

Maurice

Maurice was Israeli, his hooter brayed it,
a swarthy Punch, the world his Judy.
Monday he'd be sun-daft, manic;
Thursday smoked-out, volcanic.

Maurice was a barber in Civvy Street,
a Q.M. lance-jack in the Paras;
Tuesday (Sweeney) he'd bawl for buttons,
Friday (Todd) swop your last-week mittens.

Anyway, there was Maurice, in the A.D.S.,
one holy Monday we were lost for plasma —
Tilley-spotlit, his sleeve rolled-up,
sporting this silvoed cannula, on tap…

Old Baton Nose, a hairy pipeline,
tied up with this captured falschirmjaeger;
purring 'As one non-Aryan to another,
have this one on the synagogue, brother!'

hoping it didn't poison, was okay with Adolf —
and the Jerry grinning, loving each dark dram.
Next day, parachutist or not,
he'd have signed for the bastard, every bleeding
        drop.

'Drag'

With patrols catwalking around each other,
we'd been slack for months in casualty.
'Drag' was on again about his wife, a sort
of sexual cormorant at week-ends.
— 'Darling, me reet leg's out on t'side of bed!'
'Where's thee left then, love?' 'Out on t'other' —
when they brought-in the mine accident, —
like a toppled brazier, shot daft with holes.

You'd think he'd gone, then suddenly he'd
        breathe,
like a child almost past sobbing.
His effects were already out:
field-dressing, paybook, green envelope (holed), —
plus a few personals: photo, ring.

'Drag' was looking at them. He said:
'Some woman's going to the pictures tonight'.

Cox

'Coxey', the unobtrusive kind,
a smile in the canteen across a nap-hand,
but there always, backing somehow...
we made the same units for years that way,
on the Gold Coast then in the Paras, —
until he caught a battalion, came back.

Oh he knew me, just. 'Lo Golf' he said.
He was stretcher-propped, an undertinge of grey.
He coughed, soft, splintery,
tried to grin, achieved a centimetre, —
then his swam back: lost fish.

I wanted to go out with a flame-thrower,
cremate them where they crouched, —
so gentle, such ruin he was.

'Slim'

Slim was born near Glasgow, on a coal-mine, –
schooled to shadow trucks for what fell off –
eyes blue as a calf's, a tidy muscle,
and a jaw like a steel box.

Slim was my mate, eccentric-loyal,
used to supervise my hooking-up,
tolerate Ronard, slabs of quiet,
and parked next on parade to a thing like a
      rubbish-tip.

By canny instinct Slim was a batman,
could make a Sam Browne glisten, a cap-badge
      ring.
I knew the O.C.'s wife by her letters:
'Listen to this Golf': 'your big head between my
      breasts'.

'Did you draw my chocolate-ration, Somerville?'
'Sir!' The blue eyes would flare, astonished,
the jaw snap against such careless talk.
Later, he'd slip me a packet, new.

A lad of quiet niceties, great seams –
who else could hide a fagend knuckles out, even
when stood to his bed? – who liked booze, bints,
but loved his wife, even her sulks on principle.

Slim and I were Para cockies,
took the air together at Ranville and the Rhine;
were lucky, drew silk that sprang, –
no Roman candles, black nines.

Bounced from some rattling galley of a Douglas,
shouting as canopies wrenched and stayed,
Slim and I grew down to earth together, –
seconds, never more than that, apart.

The choice of air and its relentless canon,
the elemental company of faith;
nothing lent, all symbiotic, giving –
those could be his wings I keep upstairs.

'Nobby'

Nobby, who moved like a gentle greenfly,
is dead, they say, of a coronary.

Nonsense. He was beyond such strictures.
He leapt, feeds on roses.

BALLAD OF THE SEAGONE SCOUSE

In Scotland Road where I was born
there was a fair maid dwelling –
black-shawled and beery, from her tit
a halfcaste brat straphanging –
and barefoot kids with bottoms out,
their fingers hot with twos of chips,
hoops that wobbled, tops that skipped,
and mangey moggies choiring.

In Everton where I shot up
(with a wooden gun for a father)
it was chewinggum on fleapit seats,
Tom Mix and Rin-Tin-Tin;
fireworks through the letter-box,
stick and bin for bat and wicket,
spuds baked black in horny jackets,
and piss to sink the embers.

At Joshua Street they taught me colours,
green and orange, red, blue;
Sunday pews and Saturday altars,
roaring Anfield, Goodison;
I kicked my heart out, dinged my ribs,
looked for wounds and picked the scabs;
the only head I took to school
was Dixie Dean's, in spate.

One day the Liver Bird flapped wings,
I heard a siren call
— an old cow, lowing in the estuary —
'Valparaiso, Ecuador':
stern letters on a thrash of screws,
then flying-fish from galley-portholes,
Rio, in a reel of rum —
back, to find her belly full.

So to and fro till forty-one,
the Formby lightship come and gone,
Birkenhead there, an old tyre
charred and smoking in the sun;
that twilight, lilting round the anchor,
flames no flash of mine could shake,
the banging patch where Bootle burned
— like roses in Sefton Park.

Then forty-three, still dribbling through,
tacking, weaving, all I knew,
(but too much water there, for once)
a wolf-pack lammed me, down I stayed,
the sodden bottom of the league —
every black-shawled, wet-candled birthday
prayed-for (in the small ads)
by 'Our Mam, Big Tess, and Ed'.

ODE TO THE RIVER SEVERN

You whispered in my mother's blood
of islands where she did her loving,
martins from their black squints
fleeting round the bubbled prow, —
and woke up in my father's dying
— Salop in Salonika —
a sweaty dream from his chest dripping
like water from an oar.

You helped my uncle back from France,
a silver trophy in his skull,
and watched him drift (the odd number,
pensioned at twenty-one)...
that mooched, half-courted, potted blacks,
sank his pints (and they him),
hung out a decade, slipped, went —
head-sprawled, in a drown of breasts.

Me the minnow-boy you took
with coracles and acorn cups,
bridges arched like snapping salmon,
weir-cathedrals, lily-flaps;
my skin lived by summer lime-scent,
half-naked, swung on ropes above you,
my days were blueshot kingfishers,
each flying heartbeat, swans.

Later, teased with saucy virgins
like trim corked bottles bobbing by,
impervious to the lusty stone,
you'd swop those adolescent eves
for midnight altar-candles, gold;
coming from that holy dark
I wrote of your reflected ripples...
'wrinkles on the brow of God'.

Later still, you turned khaki
threw me to exotic sons;
I felt you louring (snakes for otters)
in the banked thunder of Gold Coast streams;
nearer, in chancy falls
of Normandy and Belgian snow;
last — a swansdown reach
of parachutes — the Rhine.

I stayed away: your rage flooded,
stood up round that left town,
halved the lampposts, lost the roads,
then clenched and set about my mother,
locked, cracked her where she lay;
irrigating what remained
found other islands, in the gut,
that pushed for dying-space (not long).

Now even, ages gone,
unlikely ever to meet again,
here, by the beck's adopted prattle,
your ghostly ambience has me still;
greedy for its every child
within my veins comes whispering too
that voice, demanding yet
the ikon of apostrophe.

Demiurge, toting the bead-heads
of Kali, the golden ladle;
eternal adept, great water-snake
whose mouthing tale is life,
when death calls in my throat
yours will be the thug-bright noose,
yours the cloud relenting over
the drycourse of my bones.

ACT OF GOD

Menageries, there the grotesque's expected.
But to have it smashed on one; human, too…
seconds after the affair find —
like some male mantis wrecked on its own lust —
the mini, half its head gone;
in the other half, canned alive,
pawing from buckled knees, through eyeless
       spectacles,
(while navvies debate about the door,
whether to unjam it with a shovel
or break new glass, try from the inside),
a man…

Picked out, draped in the ambulance he says:
'Was it a stationary vehicle I hit?'
says it four times;
then thickly, through remains of blood:
'Was there a black dog in front with me?'

No dog. Only his mother-in-law;
now blanket-ballast, all but a foot.

AT A CHECKPOINT

Look, the wire's gone. Even if
that new stuff the wall's made of
— stress-plastic slape as glass —
has no recorded melting-point
things feel easier. Anyway...

COMPLY GET BY (clench-fist-flanked)
in kingsize capitals that won't wear off.
Not exactly subliminal perhaps,
but big enough to assume, forget.
And if it saves one thinking-time...

Guards? Still up there, true
— set machine-guns, trained lights —
but pure showbiz, rather
fetching in a dated way...
almost like Beefeaters.

Internally, no complaints...
no one officially away
having their anus pried
(for microfilm, queer stains).
Quiet, that's all it really takes.

What's that dinosaur of a siren, rearing?
Those tanks rampaging from a yell of ground?
That thing in the Colonel's telescopic sights?

A girl with an arm of tulips and a love-letter
— in her own hand, too —
half a mile away...and still approaching...

PEACE WITH HUNGER

Gulls crying for wet bread,
the grass a shock of bayonets,
and where the snow's tensest
stoat's eyes...

I have written this cold poem
many times before;
yet still the bones stick out:
an old, broken corset.

SUMMER STORM

Suddenly it's all helpless —

from the doomed cruiser of the house
revving smoke, useless —

to the blindfold blossom faces:
prisoners waiting to be shot —

all headline-weather, nemesistic, normal:

a crack of pit-props in the sky.

HISTORY: A BUTCHER'S HOOK

At Pompeii the menu à la carte:
those dishy favourites canis or puella
broiled in lava, served
in a glass case.

At Capri a chap arriving
airmail, via Tiberius;
who wasn't, for an Emperor, that bad;
didn't persecute the Christians.

And at Amalfi, St. Peter (plastered)
in goitrous triumph bringing on
a child, its own small cross
already nailed.

Then Rome, Il Duce's balcony . . .
shopping later, in a sky blue
as its bovine stare,
one flayed, inverted crown.

Over the Alps even (height-shriven)
a look of creatures
in a common grave;
some few blanketed . . .

RAIN BEFORE DAWN

The boy hears it purring
like a pet electric train;
lapped in that living magic
there's no time left for day.

To the groom it's a mare's tail,
swished a moment invites again
the toe-curl of oblivion
not yet crammed into riding-boots.

The girl pours it through her fingers
— sand, sand, on a lover's thigh;
wreath-and-veiled her wishes ride
wave-born, a rainbow spray.

Only the farmer does not dream:
the dusty ploughland of his body struck
suddenly with holy running-over:
spires, miracles, a sky of corn.

NATURE NOTES

Walks by prongs. Is
divided at extremities,
unites at hairy intervals.

Haunts the Impossible Isles.
Holes in the air or ground.
Clothes by arrangement with inferiors.

Mating usually face to face.
The young born
pre-packaged, down a chute.

Moral stature indeterminate.
Food anything from God to garlic.
Offal likewise.

Self-protected. Known to kill itself.
Sometimes does this for others.
If not, death by falling-off . . .

STOCK

He shows me how he 'settles' hens
— swinging them, like a cowboy with a lariat,
round and round by the convenient neck . . .
a gag he learnt while out in Africa with
        R.E.M.E.,
from his boy, who 'knew a trick or two like
        that!'.
Most, at the fourth and final twist,
drop off quietly, with just a twitch, —
like rag-dolls lying in a white heap
by the pump-handle (disused now these many
        years).
Sometimes, it's not so easy: say
one's lost its head, not had the sense to keep
the thing a secret, but must stagger round
dramatically, with a red spike, —
as if the scene weren't modern, but some fuss
        put on
by Bloody Mary, over Tower Hill.
Once (he laughs) there was a joker
that wouldn't play, but landed right-side-up,
like a clown on a trampoline, quite intact, —
then clucked twice and tried to high-step off
as if no more had menaced
than a somersault in snow.
'Then?' 'Oh, she gave us an encore;
but muffed it, got something in her eye.
Luck like that's not meant to happen twice;
not to fell-farmers, anyway!'.

FOREWARNED

Half made up (with more zest than art,
as if for a child's party, a minstrel show)
their charcoal-smeary faces wait
my coming across new turf.
Their legs dazzle, sunlit chalk,
you can look through the pink ears,
nearer, see they've cords yet, —
wispy, like bent wire.

Then she ruckles throatily from thirty yards,
gargles them to her across the grass,
quavering like cracked oboes
they bounce into her shaggy tent;
one at each side, splayed, oblivious,
their tails wriggling like mad tadpoles.

As always in March I think:
how could that swaddled old drab
ever find such lambs —
she with the fleece of bilgewater,
that gashed horn, gammy leg.

With black-barred yellow eyes she marks me,
my pitch, smell.
Bony jaws champ sideways, quicker.
The belly's palpitant.

Beneath, they butt and gorge.
But she keeps her eyes on me,
clinching yellow eyes that say:

who's fooling who with this lyric slop?
Begin as you intend to finish, man.
Smile, show the abattoir.

THE RECIDIVISTS

The old man, indecently confined
to the barracks of his bones;
or if paroled at all, only
for a pack-drill sortie to the shop upstreet;
allowed letters, Social Security,
and (odd days) a hunched fire
whispering to itself, or like a stray cat
with maddening quietness washing, washing . . .

Or the old woman, away for life,
between bedpans blurting her yellow shame:
like some half-blind bitch interminably
            scratching
for buried amulets, a place to go —
among joke-marrows, toothmarked scraps,
and huge starched professionals that screen
her frailty with tough solicitude,
her senseless maundering with labelled flowers.

Or the swan, decoyed and killed;
its broad-arrowy web-tracks on the ice
still pointing to the river-chink
whose noose of zero strangled hope that night;
monumental now, looped, left
like soiled laundry for the washerwoman flood —
with a head, perhaps,
if one could look that far . . .

Convicted. Sentenced. But demonstrably for
          what?

What have they done, these pitiable grotesques?
What have they done but live?

ON CLEM: A CAT

A thing of piebald moods, true to his born
        colours —
querulous if shook from noonday beds
yet mornings given to nudging one awake
breathy, tickling, with stubborn tenderness . . .
not much at bouncing intruder toms
but liked to prowl for dogs, the bigger the
        tastier . . .
could saunter with a mannequin's rubato
but was never that feline about birds
save once: dozing on a sill
he snapped a breakneck bluetit rebounding off
        the pane . . .

We had him thirteen years.
Then something grew between:
he'd drool, subside in road-middles,
mess anywhere.
So, the vets. The last time
— oddly enough —
he purred like a sun-tuned grasshopper.
After, we couldn't open
that cardboard-box — all the way back
colder, heavier —
but buried him with it.

He's there, by the garden-fence,
two sticks looped over with washing-line.
A rough job . . . like death generally...
but fitting somehow (he was farm stock)
and lasts, has meaning; if not perhaps
for the robin that sometimes lingers
wind-flaked, on its cross.

NEIGHBOURS

Black-tipped ears abrupt as antlers
a hare canters past, diagonal;
its lack of haste, I like to think,
by way of compliment.

SURD

Star-manna, not a crumb impure.
Then you, Venus:
a rosette of rapiers
on the other wall.

VENUS

A gold spider claiming her silks of air;
around, the starry ruck
mere flies, bloodless.

TOAD TRACKS

Spawn

The sun, that terrifying clock, moves us —
no other.

Some, already done,
flounder into leaf waste.

Others still tout,
shout for alibis, a late flare —

while the boys scramble, nag
at mounted females harden harden

for what? This fern-slung necklace:

a thousand beady eyes on time . . .

Deadpan

Turned, your belly's soft
as blotting-paper.
I could gut you with a thumb.

But those humped eyes
gold as grain.

Primrose-leaf-backed old gargoyle
in the wild Elizabethan court-shoes

sit in my lappy hand
till it sinks, —

then swim for it, who better?

Amplexus

They say if you take a stick the same width
as a female, take it in spawning-time,
the male hasps on to it, you almost have
to break an arm to unfix him.

Look at this teak-slammed life-grapple,
this monstrous jockeying for eternity,
male bossed on female, clamped over —
you can believe it.

Eros

Spring, in all her fetching frippery —
tesselation of leaf-shadow,
the beck magpie-blue, the fall
a white mare's tail brilliant miles away . . .

Down there's a couple surfaced, sideways on:
stiffening slop-bloated dowager
with her grandson still cooing on her —
eyes glint-blind, forearms dug in —
that can't let go.

GALATEA

Those months I drew her out of native marble
— fathered on Venus in a dream of hands —
she was nearest. Finishing a thigh,
the whole torso would cleave to me,
linger, as if the touch were salve,
so deep in the emergent flesh it moved
like blood beneath. I never heard my chisel,
so absolute was our creating silence,
the powered ritual of bringing forth.

So it was strange that when it came at last
— that unbelievable confirmed waking —
the sense was splintered desolation;
as if with birth some magic caul
that bound both had torn unmendably.

Is there love between us? Between, yes.
Oh to be adult, fair to the male's vanity,
she'll tolerate: my fingers brush
resigned nipples, a courteous back . . .
but as byplay: constantly
her eyes overlook the instant grass,
to mate with pine-vistas, smoke-fingers,
a sail dipping like a butterfly far off.
She would invite, it seems, only
the ghostliest consummation:
a gilt impotence . . . of Apollo, say.

Continually now the questions, hornets.

Am I hope's cuckold, this apparition
a changeling shifted on me by her mother —
my flesh, but lost, looking
eternally for first love:
a page ripped from her pillow-diary
by some outraged priestling incarnations since?

Is she self-afraid, of the forked kiss
and its lusty consequence the human mess:
the blind head of the Other crippling
her careless triumph, remote joy?

Or is it my fault, does she probe me as I am:
pocked, scurfy, her natural father both in age, mind?
Realise all my creepy indecisiveness, a freak able
        to handle only
a mallet's precious trade?
It would be easier if the heartbeat were
        inaudible.
Stone, she belonged.

ONE UP ON CIRCE

Eve functional, pacing a sow's ear patch,
snouting for dusty truffles, squinting from
        tucked eyes
at dubious offshoots, scratching her buttocks on a
        stump, —

or Eve fabulous, lying lark-riveted;
belly taut, interleaving hair,
that cheek soft as a spring moon . . .

(Adepts both: nabbing
the handiest tree, taking what they seek
of here and Eden).

But which? The island teaser:
to be lost in luscious passion, —
or found in weathered use?

I pause to scratch a hairy hindpart,
tot points up with a cloven trotter,
state (baldly) my unparisian choice.

The grotesque.
This other could be sun-hooked, want
the fruit shaken down for her.

WOMAN OF THE PHILISTINES

Romantics visualise her flagrant,
every breath the youth of Gaza
dithyrambic about those powered breasts,
that sway of arrogance, panache.

Likelier she was bony,
scrag-chested, bloodless-seeming;
prosecuting her business in the field
so quietly it passed for casual.

Others (the curious or competitive)
had mobbed him blatantly, open-armed;
sunned themselves at the tremendous story,
lost their maidenheads like so much spoil.

This was noticeably different, —
provokingly indifferent, you'd say.
In a look he'd felt anomalous;
locks straggly, the famous beard untrimmed.

So deftly was it managed. Intrigued, he had to
      follow,
take her home, pay court just more than
      flippantly;
and once within that sweaty cave lie conquered,
meat for nature, her leonine necessity.

Not merely in the throes of midnight either,
when her mouth was a tongue-lashed whirlpool
      sucking down,
but often through the day's drag when
housewifely she'd rummage round,

confiscating, putting-by, —
the club draped unmindfully, the pelts
where the ledge curved, not a sly bone
to bite-on, a pink scrap . . .

deadliest when she was 'mother', killing
charitably, with devout concern;
stealing his loincloth for the wash, tucking him
        up for days,
compliant, warm . . .

All in all, he stuck it decently, the months
of marrow-draining, pampered sloth;
the timed meals of herbs and flattery,
the questions nagging at strength, strength.

Yet at last capitulated, sabotaged
completely by her triple mutability;
gave up his otherness, his maned truth,
to wake strangely rested, in foreign arms.

Here, captivity was kinder, chains
predictable, not intertwined
with serpentine wet-leathery solicitudes,
thigh-smooth promises and pieties.

It was worth it, to feel again
with hairy hands the pillars' cold integrity;
able, in the roaring hall,
the hard male voices he could understand,

to fight directly, without humbling love.
Sensual trappings, ritual sport, —
hurling them to that night they'd brought upon
        him
he may, even, have embraced the loss.

PLACINGS

Ascot

Daisy: trompe l'oeil:
a fried egg sporting
a late-Comanche headdress.

Gorbals

Daisy: small sunface
remembered meanly
by the cold, knife-throwing moon.

Tyburn

Laburnum rampant:
sun-gallows on which time hangs
its brilliant rebels.

Bannockburn

Platoon of thistles:
dram-battened Jocks, all tossed tams
and jagged bottles.

Farnborough

The sky vapour-trailed:
Picasso, drawing
with a flashlight, photographed.

COMMAND PERFORMANCE

Quizzed by the evening star,
a visiting mikado
whose moustaches drip —

a moon crude
as a wax banana
takes its twangy
blackbottomed bow.

SUMMER SCHOOL

Take the use out, reclaim the poetry.
So, slopping about deliciously unkempt
in clottish aprons, sniffing turps
like ozone or a breath of cowslip
sidled-in upon some offbeat breeze,
so this flush of matrons, for a weekend
away from husbandly quirks, childish nose-
        bleeds,
bills, barneys, hems for stitching,
limpet relatives, the drilling 'phone,
dabs, mauls, swipes away
for the sting of it, the tang of what could
        come . . .
wreaking their sinister collages
of chipped chimney-cowls, bed-knobs,
apprehensive laths, hanks, scraps . . .
titivating the Old Unquenchables,
nudging the subconscious for a buckshee myth,
splicing old rope and garter-ribbon, trailing
tossed clues of line or bevel . . .
in none of this companionable fury
for one faithless, irrecoverable moment
less than solid, sensible.

For this perhaps is it: reverting to convert:
the operative thing no longer pat
occasion squeezed into an oily gloss,
but matter thinking for its fugue-self:
possibles, organic dares,
impromptu gambits, thrills of apposition,
meetings, matings, chancy flares,
some sudden gorgeous resolution.
And if impulse twists the arm unhandily
or blind elaboration overlays, well,
it was there once, among the other right
inseparable shapes, and could amaze again . . .
tomorrow, now.

GLADIOLUS

Some will shiver, break style
at a vase-movement,
a cat's breath.
With you, nothing drops:
from leaf-pinnacle
to bud-tangent
so pointed up
– placed, held,
overlapping –
the spine of sheer art's
less obvious with every bloom:
lost in the last,
that takes the air
like a great dandy's scarf,
so sure.

FREE SKATING CHAMPION

We have seen those osprey-gliding voluted arms
sow on a gift of music instant hellebore,
turning the bald glacier into gyroscopes of bloom.

Have seen that lariat body make of air
whirlpool calyces, corollaries spun
lightnings after, rooted and away . . .

Seen feet, bladed winds,
from all points of your compassing converge:
a typhoon axis whizzing past itself . . .

coming out crescendo-cool,
to break slow as a Japanese water-flower
into curtsied perianth.

And here you stand, superbly casual,
in the screech of arc-lamps, the cloudburst acclamation —
as if Persephone came with the rest of it;

nature, would happen anyhow.

PROSPECTING THE RESERVES

Certain things seem now definite.
Those urgent vacuums that sucked at youth
— muscled currents against which tensed
and wrestling sharply you found yourself —
these are lost, irrevocable.
And even if the rains came again, and saw
you midstream, booted to the brash thighs,
whipping a new rod, with tactics for the
        crannies —
your cast would be gammy-handed, your net
too frayed, irreparable by magic.
You could not hold by any sleight
the fly-snap silver of ambition or of ecstasy —
even if such salmon came near enough
they'd play with you before contemptuously
        vanishing.

What is there left then?
A droughty trickle,
in a stony make-do bed;
sun-chopped, off white.
But with compensations clearly mapped:
no random terrifying splashes to report,
no fancy naiads ogling to sour reeds,
never a burbling shallow, gruesome deep.
And on the positive, what gentle gains:
an easier look at others still in spate;
a head for the stream's history, its wrinkles,
        quirks;
what eddies snub, what rapids crab
the preened ebullient challenge . . .
freedom to judge with dispassion, tact;
to slough the personal, survive in acts, objects . . .
perhaps, even, a late spring . . .
wand-flicked, from land thought salt-dry.

TENURE

On a concrete beam below the last bridge
— one of those eyebrow efforts leaving the village
where the lorries open their screeching throttles
at a straight sight of highway —
there's a dipper's nest.

I like it, like to think
of the hard artefact underpinned
by that hairy vaginal pull;
of birds sexing the numb stone;
coming, coming at will...

Three eggs. Before feeling them again
I dip my fingers in the racy font;
hoping to rebaptise the human touch;
blessing their beak-tenacious folly, praying
when dawn breaks it brings a future . . . eyes.

ALL I CAN SAY

1   *Mouths, Words*

ANSWERING THE CHILD

Did the wind kill its mother?
Not yet. Tomorrow.

Can the sun burn itself?
Only so you can't see.

Will the moon freeze?
That's how the sun left it.

Will the ice break?
Only your heart.

END OF A CAT

I was away that weekend.
They'd kept her for me,
in a newspaper, sellotaped.

I unwrap her,
unwrap death.
A stiff leg hits me first,
then fourteen years of weeping.

'Christ. Christ'
is all I can say.

I do not believe in Christ.
Only my need believes —

my need a god
whose agony understands.

NO MORE

How does one ritualise a cat's death?
With the misnomer of violin-strings
miaouling, wailing?

Or a wake of sardine-portions
rolled lavishly round the mouth,
each morsel a salivating, velvet memory?

One ritualises a cat's death
by drinking milk, purely.

SNAILS

stroll daintily
on many paths

their seashell
houses with them

cut pretty silhouettes
out of leaf-green

quiz with eyes
ferruled on tentacles

leave wakes
that take a day to die

are whanged
on thrush-anvils

crushed
by casual boots

us

SLUGS

seem not to move
but do

seem not to have
the guts to mate

(yet deep grass
finds them glued, oozy)

seem lifeless
but for the way they cling

like drying tar
to anything that touches . . .

leeches black armbands
stigmas liabilities

never very far away from
blood

SNAIL THRUSH

You fell from heaven.
A spotted waistcoat,
long legs,
bright eyes.

Your knock was stony.
You broke, entered,
scooped,
ate me whole.

Chips of my armour
strew the concrete;
light as your next
footfall.

WOODPECKER

The last wing-spluttered pigeon has left
and croons far-off like French horns.
The hooligan jays cranking their football-rattles
are drunk somewhere else.
And that girlish drawing-room soprano of a linnet
laid away in Victorian album-leaves.

Lean the back of your head against a trunk.
You can be quiet now, civilised, hear
the drumtap artery at your skull.

BLOODED

We had come down from the wood, our eyes still
with the peacock tails of tree-twilight.
An occasional beetle went twanging past
like some celestial tuning-fork, going to a moon
laid in its sky-salver like a fuzzy apricot.
We had resumed the car, were bumping down
the track, in an estuary of moored sheep
— ghostmoths rising obliquely at our headlamps —
when we saw the fox — our first — and stopped.
Strangely, it didn't vanish.
It was twice a cricket-pitch away —
like a yard of mist, triangular-faced,
floating its tail out level as its bodiless body . . .
It was the night perhaps, so bland
things were content within it, to be, do nothing else.
And no wind, any scent would go
straight to heaven, innocuous as smoke.
Anyway, there it was: messing about
inhaling what happened: dust, dew.
Twice it looked at our dimmed headlamps,
but without interest;
it had one moon, harvest enough.
And once almost came down the road . . .
then veered, rummaged some more,
without looking again leapt a wall.

We thought we could still see it; after minutes
of stood breath decided it was stone.
So went on.
Not happiness, but the way it sidled,
would stay the memorable thing.

A half-creature, less workable than dog,
less mob-impregnable than pure wolf,
that in time — the hunter's moon —
someone would kill . . .
not for doing what anyone might,
but — unforgivably — looking guilty about it.

EWE

You will be born wherever it takes her:
by the wall, under barbed-wire,
excreted in a splurge, left
in a ruck of oakleaves to stumble up,
cakewalk to a smell of nipple —
a draggled ha'porth with a bellrope tail
and suds of wool on you.

You will grow on swerves of hillside
flanked by the profiled ash, stampeding plover,
where larks rummage the heather, rooks surf-ride wind.
These you will not notice.
Leather-legs you will.

You will obey three people:
your mother, Fang (panting about
your ankles) and
Leather-legs, who brings you
different food.

You will have good times: sun-tucked
or in a patch of sweeter grass;
with your fleece a white rock
of sea-anemones, wind-slurred;
or as the starling likes to preen you,
straddled on your nappy back...
even harmony, your feet raining
with the flock's down twisty lanes,

your voice riding a slope of air
to the ring of pail-handles
in the field below;
even your brand-mark will at times look
like a mere cosmetic, modish, gay . . .

Sometimes you will finish early, dropping on a gun.
Then, your name will be lamb.
Others, your luck may stretch
to a double syllable: mutton.

Or they may think you good for young:
one of your uncut brethren play a strange leapfrog stopped
at a place you never knew you had:
you unwittingly brooding
that potent lightning till one day
you're restless yourself, haunt the wall,
grunt with flared nostrils baring your teeth
then with the same groan as your dam's blurt
amazingly into wet life . . .
in a few minutes bumping along
your belly weak as a drunk while you
impassively clear up, gobbling the yellow slack,
maybe a mouthful of oakleaves with it . . .

They will say you do not need your coat such bland weather
and give it away for you.
Should you be blessed with fine young
they may save you, hoping for yet finer.
Granted always the long inertia of parasites you may munch on
into middle-age, letting it all happen,
chewing the gummy cud, the cud always,
through other births, routine lessenings . . .

And one day, you will not be:
perhaps painlessly assimilated;
perhaps lost somewhere in hillside grass
like a barrel pitched from a lorry, burst;
perhaps a skull even, horn-hooked over
a branch of ash, sex-and-eyeless . . .
swinging play for the sharp-beaked
catapulting wind.

A life not too unusual, in fact.
If it's a help, and you can, remember
no one will do a thing for you
they wouldn't for one of your own.

TOTEM ANIMAL

The day, windless. Ninety yards ahead
a leaf long as a Spanish chestnut's
idly traverses the road;
sudden, climbs a wall.
Rare, but could be . . .
I brake, peer over, make kissing noises
(stoats are curious, they say).
But he's not for games like that —
head-prods out of a dark slit
then with a look, a lightning give-away —
white slash of throat, body slung
like a racing-car's, blowpipe dart of a tail —
bucks off along the wallside, in a rage
at interruption when the blood's set,
or rancour at the scent
of human trespass on his flushed preserves.
Whatever, I don't pursue . . .
but in the hot mirror, miles on,
boring at me with black pupils,
find a new face, skinhead-sure.
Sudden, the world's a skidding
blood-squeal, a rabbit throat.

ENIGMA

The new moon —
a stopped boomerang —
the gate,
and the skyline mare —
back dipped
like the sheepwall
she stands by
(only smoother) . . .

In the sunset's
casual apricot
why does she turn
and look at me —
who am not
beautiful?

REBUKE

I am at the gate.

You stand etched in sunlight,
then slowly canter down;
wind ruffling the russet nap
of your coat, turning
your mane spiky.

What do you want?
Love or apples?

I stroke, you toss your head,
show hail a lip, teeth.

Love, I have no apples.

You stretch, obstinate,
nip my shirt.

What's love
but a giver of apples?
your silence says.

CAGED

The animals who can't laugh haunt me —
the puma's padding, silent snarl;
the wild ass circling gently with her forefoot,
while her barred mate lengthens his drooling shaft;
the dazed lion roaring out of stupor
like someone with shrapnel in his gut —
the animals who can't laugh haunt me —
mouths, wounds.

SHORE PICKINGS

The edible crab:
a Cornish pasty trying
to pinch its own crust.

Flatfish pebble-slurred:
memorial brasses not
for deciphering.

The lissom conger's
sinuous parade, water
its body-stocking.

The octopus, hunched
like an owl or trailed downwave,
a probing dahlia.

Sail of a yacht, leant
out of history: a quill
deft at wave-psalters.

The oyster-catchers:
slate-chippy cries, chevroned wings,
scuttling from flicked spray.

The stranded starfish
left in a lunatic rush —
a glove inside out.

A shorn hermit-crab;
its new pad like a topi
dragged over its head.

Some prawns, perspex-frail:
anatomy lessons, toy
X-rays of themselves.

The storm rodeo:
Stetson-slapping winds busting
the buck of combers.

Cormorant flying.
Night on day, drab assassin
of the fish's dream.

The wreck's reminder:
a mast stabbed like a hatpin
into sunset's heart.

Twilight cormorant:
trumpeter of nemesis,
clinching a last post.

2   *The Truth of It*

LAMENT FOR PROPHETS

We have liquidated myth and image,
the lucid east, creative stable.

No voice from thunder any more,
no oracle, poignant smoke.

Now, we send folk
to the moon to imagine it;

supermarketing, come home
to battered, hairless dolls.

FOR VERNON WATKINS, CUM GRANO SAILS

Next day awakening's with a new line:
'Light between leaves: a crushed gold.'
Something you might have dreamed, on that cliff edge
of miracle, about your copious head
a white gull of glory, and beyond,
Christ The Word, striding blue-sandalled
the wind-flecked breakers of Rhossili bay.

Through you, out of me: a strange coupling.
And, conning the text once more, I wonder.
'Light between leaves': you, yes . . .
but 'crushed', never: unless the term express
– distilled in some metaphysical retort –
not moral bruising but residual humility . . .
platonic essence (heavenly oil, in short).

'Heavenly.' There no doubt the thread:
your holy Muse, communion of poets,
resurrection by breath, and myth everlasting –
these dead that touch, their vaulting agonies;
foal, unicorn, saint, samaritan . . .
beloved accidents, affinities that make
out of a line's gold cord another, singing world.

So, what can I say to such transcendent certainty?
Try the realist cure, a dash of salt Perhaps?
Useless. Over that sea-shoulder
it could turn to wisdom, supernatural luck.
Against the chary grain though it glint then, this blessing.
Gentlest of wizards, ply your spells —
in leaves of rapture, gold.

THE VANDALS

Once more we had the wood surrounded. Where blue
house-smoke had trickled yelling we charged.
To stop, stupidly.
The door was wide, contemptuous.
Worse, there were no booby-traps.

They must have smelt our purpose, slipped the noose
last night, some cryptic way, —
their children briefed, their bright incredible
ikons wrapped against the roving moon.
We had the freedom of their indifference, now.

The halo-drifted air, the pressing text,
grace of absolution, communicable bread, —
all that we'd resolved to loot and lose,
vanished. For crucial nails
picture-marks, unfleshed stigmata; gaping, dry.

So here we sit, morose, leaderless,
picking at knife-handles, desperately cocked
for the next wind of its magnetic settling:
the stanchless chapel-cup of mad legend
still glintingly inviolate.

And with what end to such compulsive piracy?
Marches, marches, circlings, waits . . .
storming of woods, abandoned houses . . .
further, barer, till starvation grips, we make
last bestial suppers of each other?

No. This wood's the last.
We must walk out individually, each
to stack and burn his weaponed heart.
Then, beneath a white flag
of certain cloud, return in time
to build a silence, kneel, it seems.

Naked, we may surprise a saviour,
hold the stouped blood, be still.

MESSIAH

When does ice move with the stream?
His hand was supple, warm.

How does wind shake out of air?
I felt, floated on his kiss.

Was there nothing, then a star?
The sky opened, grew within.

When does moonlight become rain?
His pupils went black, he died.

JESTING PILATE

'Christ, not here again!'
groans somebody behind,
and out of a brown habit
jabs the begging-box,
and the skullcapped
whiteroped friar
with a five-tongued prayer
on a small card:
'Pax Et Bonum';
'May His Face
Be Always Towards You' . . .
and one thinks
(caught again)
what's the truth
of it and Him?

The mad carpenter
with the mouth full
of greedy nails —
or the gentle saviour
who did not ask
but found disciples —
whose working hands
were five-tongued psalms,
an everlasting
pentecost of birds?

NO BRASSARDS, YOU'LL GIVE THE BATTALION AWAY

'— and Ronnie was climbing a wall.'
Ronnie, that modest, witty man,
who'd said: 'Swop the flash —
from Pegasus to crossed spades?' —
Ronnie was climbing a wall.

No one should make jokes about war.
Bullets can climb, too.

PROOF

Rusty used to say
I was dead lucky.
I could never see it,
till it stared
from the shell dressing
that was Rusty's face.

SIBLINGS

Both, at times, sounded
almost human.
Bombs would cry for one
all the way down,
quite operatic tears.
Shells were equally demonstrative,
only gay:
streamlined to a point
they'd come at you
swanking about it.
Considering the final,
faceless impact,
it all seemed
somewhat odd.

ONE FOR THE LORD

'This'll be bang on, back in the line;
the boys'll do more for one of their wounded, y'know.'
That was Colonel Dobson (of Dobson's Force)
— a spirited atheist Regular —
boasting a bandaged hand, less one finger.

God moves, they tell us, in mysterious ways.
Was it to boost conversion, puff morale,
reprove psychology, or a Trinitarian mix?
Anyhow, the following week
he'd his foot blown off.

SOFT MICK

'When He sees fit to take me, I shan't mind.'
So Mick the believer, who'd no more wear
a tin hat than a flowered pisspot,
but ambled everywhere bald and beautiful,
and would sleep in a cot of salvoes,
religiously unimpressed.

And whether the Lord had a touch of strabismus,
or the charisma of that stately pleasure-dome
turned the airy heads of bullets —
but Mick stumped back to Civvy Street
with a faith bigheaded as the Eddystone lighthouse —

and the Lord isn't fit yet.

INITIATION

A girl of seventeen,
chopped by a mortar flake,
throwing the blanket off
her naked breasts,
moaning in shrapnel French
'Denis . . . Denis . . .'.

I was a virgin then,
would ease her down
lingering on the flesh,
hoping she'd rise again —

trying to mask desire
by taking her pulse, remarking
on her sweaty brow,
anything clinical but sex . . .

not fooling for one heartblink
the Colonel — a gynae man
in Civvy Street —
who knew it down to the last
vaginal wrinkle.

'Where she's got it, she's lost.'
So much for virgins, both.

HEIRLOOMS

The stoup I stole as victim,
from an abandoned Belgian house.
With its head of Christ looking like silver
it lurched with me through to Dunkirk,
shot at, ransomed by the pigswill fog,
to end hung up at home.

The gun was presented to me as victor
by a German Oberleutnant:
an automatic, small and sweet
as a toy, a handshake.
From the Baltic, where its taut
dainty incentive first touched me,
it came in time to the same house,
aired for visitors.

Post-war, I gave each away —
the stoup to a lame Catholic,
the gun to someone
crossing the Sahara.

Both became enemies.

OBITUARIES

This one barked regardless, bit to kill.
Here, seemed brashly to invite
his putting-down, the dry deletion made
at eight sharp upon a morning walk.

This one fawns and lives, yet in
that agony of caution's hung
failure gross as any slung
snake-throated on the dark.

OPERATION USURPER

The King must not be hurt.
There must be no smuggled notes hinting
the Court is less than pleased
with the Royal Person, or that the Queen survives
on dark yens for beefy scullions below.

The King is still the King.
Daubs, seditious mimicry,
baleful writing on the jasper walls, —
such will not be countenanced. Nor any
sudden-tongued eunuch to suggest
that crowd beyond the gates roars
for anything but draggled captives.
Or that God, in time, will not reply . . .
(granted always an official invitation).

All confidants have been screened, briefed.
The generals have never been so close;
not one with detectable friends in hemlock.
That muted hammering you hear is only
the People's secret birthday-gift:
a carved wooden effigy of Himself
for propping in the city-square . . .
tinder-dry, to fit their burning love.

The King is still the King.
When you fail to wake him on the Day remember
the King must not be hurt.

MARTYR

Yellow-robed, on cathedral steps,
under the whine of jets, where tanks stalk,
the spit of Jesus, of any man,
with no shade but truth, I burn.

Burn for a thought, a stake in freedom,
speech between humans, a common loaf;
this roaring pride, that raging end,
your pure asbestos, life.

Hear my black flesh. Begin.

NIGHT CALL

Someone is using the code down there: three buzzes, then off, on.
Someone is jamming twopenny tears into the slotted void of your
        coming —
obscenely tearing up sleep's road with a ravenous pneumatic drill.

Did you imagine for one star-brash moment you could hold joy
        intact?
You must go down in your lovesweat, stand shivering in the hall,
        take it.
Someone is on to you down there. Someone has the code.

WAKING

My hair was blond. I had a third finger.
Where have I been, that changes it?
Why this stone in my clenched hand?
The smell of burning feathers on my tongue?
What is this glass I walk through, breathless,
this other, silent glass?
Did I write to God? Have I a name?
I want to say something. Whose voice will come?
There is an eye in the turret of my forehead.
It moves. Ask it.

VILLAGE CHURCH: CAPO DI SORRENTO

An altar bursting with cherub-heads,
and from the Babe crooked in the Virgin's arm
a yoyo string whose limit finds
— stopped heartbeat of music — a bell.
Baroque. Its inspired bathos
— promiscuous, appalling, healing —
no more refusable than a high-chaired
jam-sticky infant waving a spoon at you,
to come and get it.

VILLAGE CEMETERY

A few veterans still come —
Sundays, maybe, to cut grass
or set vases upright, fill
with flowers, water
from the long-necked can
kept in the porch.

There are the rooks, of course,
that were here before Christ —
pivotal nests smudging the elm tops —
and the occasional visitor taking in
cherubs, angels,
rain-gouged dates.

Perhaps an emigré
stopped by from Australia —
trying to speak
to a knelt boy in a bedroom;
a sense of tears on the wind,
of withered berries

but ruin mostly:
unfurnished graves
(some without headstones, even)
low as ramps on a road,
that one doesn't see
till one's almost on them —
a slight, tyre-worrying
nudge, in and on the way.

GERANIUM SUMMER

A pony rubs
the wood of a gate,
shapes to a caress
what began in flies.

Sun-tempted,
in a lane beyond,
imperceptibly almost
a fern unties . . .

and higher,
across green-gold,
a heron saunters,
a curlew cries.

In the street,
the still heat,
a slipped petal
gently lies:

heaven,
in a moment held
immediate
as eyes.

JULY FIELD

Marguerite, sorrel, vetchling: so charged, subtly beautiful
you want to find the heart, die into it.
But how? Possess by rape?
Though your tousled exits seem like spokes to circled truth,
not so: you lost when first you trod.
Nor is magic valid: drunk on ladybird's blood,
under grassblade spire and buttercup gantry,
however brave your tiny scarlet tabard
you could only do what the town does,
socialise a mystery.

Better embrace the real. There is no heart,
no centre for the questing, pinpoint eye,
no cause to probe.
More important, no need for such.
Look at the wind instead, how those spectral dolphins
move downfield like the hands of a masseur . . .
till the thing's toned like a single muscle,
vibrant, in ravished play.
Be that wind. Sense, accept . . .
nothing but the suppliant whole,
the green expansive gift, no end
to its clover-scented gorgeous flowering . . .
only perfection: in its ripe time
the scythe of Shiva, death.

THE OPTICS OF HOLISM

To split the eye three ways, see
conclusively the wind turn
a sycamore leaf to a white star,
a silver birch to a corral of manes,
yet in the same flashed breath defer
to the branched indifference of a clock —
this is spontaneously to cry
for single dedication: either
to kneel down before the hope of Light,
ride the wild present like a brave, bareback,
or settle for design in
Roman inches, equably . . .

Yet, to be whole, one is required to conjure
all three, expressly fuse
their grained autonomies . . .

Difficult. Yet, imperative to keep
mid-eye its blazing possibility;
in a star-spurred second
the heart's unearthly centaur
giving immortal presence
to the timed, pragmatic hoop.

And though such triple magic's
the unlikeliest constellation —
to practise is to look.

STREET

Suddenly all the upstairs windows
— like the ports of a man-of-war —
are open, primed for a fifty gun salute.
It's April again, as usual, bang on —
and all of us, fools together.
Though the grass is tintack-short
somebody's uncle tries shirt-sleeves and a mower.
Somebody's nephew is legs beneath a car,
somebody's dad retouching an Edwardian gas-lamp.
A dowager in a bun and stout shoes
trundles her spike-tailed dachsie

parkwards — so lowslung
it seems to run on castors.
Girls bouncing a ball and skipping
shout 'Hey, the dingdong man'
and cluster for tubs, comets.

The bus driver at the road end
sings to his chiming change
and flirts with somebody's granny.
A housewife takes the pegs out of her mouth
and talks spring sales over the garden fence;
glaring meanwhile at a perched starling
she thinks could blot her sheets
A mongol clasps his knees and rocks,
crows, grins, on a lawn.
Coming towards me are two boys:
one fuzzyheaded as a plane tree bobble,
waving a green ice buy banner;
the other, white, destroying a wafer.
Lick, bite, feel the bright delicious cold
grip your teeth, bite on, through.
Suck your fingers, as quickly, forget.

DEFINITIVE

A gust blows winter on us.
'Catch one, you'll be lucky!' you cry;
prancing at the bonanza dizzily
swooshed from bucket-grey.

The wonder is, you still do it
— as if the world that second began —
an infant who never walked
till snowflakes happened. Then, ran.

TWO RIDDLES AND A PROVERB

Rises snake-charmingly from leafy baskets,
ticks like a robin, spits like a cornered cat.
Lish as a squirrel mizzles up trunks of nothing,
snores into sloth, volcanic overhang.
Is eighteenth-century, a powdered wig;
any century, a dusty flag;
suddenly pregnant, billowy-mad;
then shapeless, evasive as a squid.
Stretches a sunny dewdrop, paints the wind,
somersaults mid-ocean over its other man,
is prancing djinn and toppling rick,
crow's-nest warning, squaw's headache.
Trips in a maze, all ends and bungle,
fades in the fist (but can smother, strangle).
Elastic metaphor, a visual pun,
may be seen through, reflected on . . .
alive, a thinskinned ghost;
dead, its own solid.

Dozes with one eye open wary as a dog,
is a harum-scarum, dabhand at tig,
can look blue as breadmould, sanguine as the sun,
tipped with the odd copper turn bilious-green.
Flashes to airy opulence, a gold-leafed thistle,
hilts for the fun of it, a belly-muscle,
hides loaded origins (seamy past
and slippery future) with instant mist.
Blurts into starry flight, the sudden lyric,
lives with wooden soldiers in a cardboard barracks
(one of whom, grazed, loses his head, blacks out);
can be more than tender in a bedsit.
Seems bright enough, but chews straws like a yokel;
constant, yes, but as swiftly, fickle.
Loves to summarise, dotes on a clean précis,
likes an ending that's snappy, saucy;
whips your coat off slick as sin
and signs the balance: skeleton.

3　*A Latrine in Purgatory*

BEDSITTERS

Lack goes into Number One,
gives the man in the mirror a lefthand smoke,
puts on hi-fi, a gas-ring,
dances with an empty coat.

Lack goes into Number Two,
cleans clean silver, cements her face,
at ten sharp kills the light —
with it, the human race.

Lack goes into Number Three,
to blackheads, a girlie magazine;
licking over the breasted pages,
sticky, afraid that he's insane.

Lack goes into Number Four,
drops her pension-book, wonders where;
looks for bedsocks, winged heels,
sits down, darns a pair.

Lack has a master-key, goes
into any number, any time,
in the house, the house that Lack builds —
wealthy as the tomb.

THREE STAR

Macaroni in green velvet
the Countess sits alone

with the head waiter's
Christian name

a voice honed
like a peacock's

a sense the game's
somehow off this year

the candle in its goblet
red as a hurricane lamp

the life she's left
yawning in her face

like a hole in the road

ANACHRONISM

You come to us escorted by a boy,
a relative, whom you bully.
You talk of women with long legs,
yellow hair, and a taste for whisky.
Only your profile looks like you, now.
Performing verse is an absurdity, we gather:
the poem's an intimate occasion,
to be whispered only, between sheets.
The boy says 'No more whisky, only wine.'
Why are you doing it then, such miles from home?
'Out of kindness to an old
family retainer: Money, of course.'
Amused, listening, we swallow truth —
poetry's bled from the locks of the Medusa,
your last book was bound in human flesh,
only the French write poems with logic —
they have no poems to write.

Are you the act? Or is the act you?
Someone with grey hair goes by you, to the bar.
'Come here, young man' you call.
Your voice is a brush of twigs over stone flags.
The boy wails 'Oh give him his whisky then.'
Someone jogs your sleeve. Your fag erupts.
'God, God, I am a mountebank' you cry.
'Burn. Burn.'
You'd like to go down as your poems do,
a fallen angel, a fighter pilot,
gabbing defiant flame —
but your sticks of bone don't merit hell,
too wet to catch hang round your sackcloth flesh
like a latrine in purgatory,
the only one in that immense bleak
interminable field.

ROMANTIC

She will never learn, devoutly spoiling
for some Caribbean of contagious youth,
some never-never coastline where the flesh
— sun-rafted, sea-hammocked —
colossally can celebrate:
between half-closed lids iridescent images
like magic carpets dawdling through . . .
or the tails of lyre-birds, voluted, fabulous.

She will never learn that even there
the brilliant paintwork blisters, bleeds;
socks sweat, the strange unforgivable
hairpin shakes out behind the bed;
the seapath's pebble-chopped; any day
the quick can fester, crabs come.

She will never learn the double edge of taking:
what's forever grasped is not the sensual gleam
but its bony inference (that such might be
time's sacrament, the stuff of charity,
seems parson's doubletalk; involved, dry).

That the gaudy drug's its own emetic
she will not appreciate: swamping each
miscarried rapture in a hogshead dream
fearfully she suffers, but must barfly on
to lusher backdrops, the same again.
Her appetite's for chronic ignorance: now
she'll never, never learn.

FORESHORE

'Glass of grapefruit?' you'd grin.
What you died of was less than cordial:
a ghostly parasite like a mad ventriloquist
gut-sewn, griping —
making you ask yourself 'More?' 'More?',
replying even as lips parched,
twitchy laughable hands complied.

What you poured yourself was not grapefruit
but dream: the ghost of a ship in an empty bottle
that would sail your drought away
but never did, next morning lost
in a tangled spew of corks, deadheads . . .

till there was no hangover, next morning
was a white cliff looking drily down.

LILY OF THE VALLEY

Like a lamp on a stair,
a whiff of porcelain . . .

Is it my drunken hand,
or the apprehension
of virginity,
that trembles?

NASTURTIUMS

Harlots

flushed importunate
in a mist
absinthe-green

their trailed
kinky limbs
nylon-sprayed

on high stools
on dead spiders
their seed bitter

TRAVELLER'S JOY

He used to date me once a week,
a salesman, staying overnight.
He lived out time for this, he said.
I was (he said) his Fate.

He came when I was lonely,
we'd meet and he'd get lit,
then arm-in-arm tiptoe upstairs.
He called me his 'expenses chit'.

He'd worked the business up himself
— nylons, quite a range;
also (sideline undisclosed)
hearts, in part-exchange.

He said he loved my swirl of hair,
that funny dimple.
I took it like a baby pap.
It was that funny, that simple.

Capsuled in a long embrace,
rocketed to outer space,
I'd wander weightless as a star,
while he slipped back, into the bar.

Oh no he never used a sheath
— 'blasphemous, they murder passion.'
Who was I to snub the Pope?
Who was I to ration?

I was more to him, he cried,
than rubies, his whole life.
I couldn't really check on it;
I hadn't met his wife.

That night I told him how I was
he went off like a gun.
'Your baby', he wrote (no name, address)
... 'after all, who led me on?'

It won't be done with senna,
it won't be worked with gin,
and I can't run home to mother, —
she'd call it sin.

So give Prue my nylon nightie,
and Jane my flowered bra;
I'm off to Septic City
where the stabhags are.

BITCH

With wives of 'possibles' she's matey, frank
about mutual headaches such as husbands, ties;
with the right children, devoutly in attendance
quite a second mother in the fury of her enterprise.

Yet somehow, the knowledge that she's unhappy
gets to reach him (the next upon the list);
let slip in some astute, unguarded moment
when grief came terribly, too handsome to resist.

Primed, limed, he can't but sympathise;
discover, dreamily, her eyes are blue;
listen when, with head half-turned away,
she whispers: 'O, if he'd be different . . . like you!'

But she can't leave him. 'Impossible, my dear.
He needs me. That cross is mine for life!'
(Besides, she might remarry, could become
that crab of rectitude, a constant wife.)

The game sharpens. Hypersensitive, he learns
the secret's open, what the others say;
and meets, in mirrors of suspicion,
shapes that mouthing turn his temples grey.

Or desperate, in the pawnshop of her heart
pays high retainers for the ghostliest of pecks;
not knowing his incandescent angel
brazen-cold, below the classic neck.

The men fight, of course. Then see her genius strut
from subtle rutting into character;
nail-varnished with the bloody lees
from midnight-scuffled fur.

But it never gets so far it cannot end
'with the happiest memories' (on her side);
and a breathing-space, perhaps, going back
to her 'true self', when she was 'just a bride'.

THE CHILDREN

Bursting in kneading their sleep-tight eyes
how will they, can they understand, the children,
the naked stranger bulking their father's place —
hairy unfamiliar shanks hard as splints against their own.
Or the rumpled girl with too wide a smile,
trying, believing she can reach them.
No clues engage, only involuntary hints:
a silent stare over half-built Lego,
a touch of shrillness, a new fad —
some outrageous trivial request
blindly stuck at, even through tears.
Already, they are caught: the only
serious question answered, gone:
how to save their crucial innocence
for the act that spawned them: love.

FIDELITY

Thrashing fresh loins,
taking revenge for a lover,
the abandoned wife rides
fiercely, in spiteful joy.

Coil-strangled,
weeping for a live
half-brother,
her children die.

STATISTICS: 2 A.M.

Lights, always. One that's suddenly risen —
like a whale's eye, with its dark hill;
one that stays on, at the top of a drive —
(propositional, boasting ruled frames);
the one that's never off, in the highrise office block
— a depthless rectangle of strip;
the very faint one, no more than a smoulder, over there —
that one keeps thinking can't be light
but diffused from some kind of heater.

It would suit to believe such lights are innocent:
a child with a smuggled torch, mending
tomorrow's scamped verbs;
a woman going down to fasten
a nagging latch;
a couple off early, while roads are clear;
a porter emptying wastebins.

Statistics are never innocent:
any month among its starlit quota
the child battered with drunken tears;
the woman touching a spot on her tongue, retching;
the couple screaming across the bed, naked;
the bankrupt, gun in mouth, preparing
to action-paint the wall.

NON-ACCIDENTAL INJURY SLIDES

Mostly it happens in the first year.
Tender flesh, hardened lash.

This was a belt. Two marks —
the smaller the buckle.

This one was strangled. You can't tell;
bruising was inside.

This horseshoe bite needs checking,
against family mouths.

Cigarette burns, these.
Get to them quickly, they fade.

Space — repeat — space your X-rays.
Fractures can be shy.

These children are briefed never
to say a thing. That is, if they can speak.

These children won't cry.
Only their wounds are attention-seeking.

These children are watchful.
What they have seen, they see.

ODALISQUE EXTRAORDINARY

Can I survive this bed, this crucial litter
of steroids, chocolates, toilet-rolls?
This view of thrush-winkled shards,
of poppies cracking into blood?

For no impressive reason this is me:
a one-girl seraglio under house-arrest:
pet, pride of that ghostly sadist
the sultan, who by threatening castration
(and for the holy kingdom of pain's sake)
has my husband as acting eunuch,
and me daily titivated
by one or other of his handmaidens:
cuffed efficient ghouls
who caliper-straighten, powder my suede boot,
tuck bedsore into sweat-crease, do me up
in moonglossed nylon nighties
(for that virgin-extra kick),
then slake my laughable human lust
with a glass dildo, a female pisspot.

Can I contain his whimsy, that cares for floozies
purged yet provocative;
when he's resting, ironic, swops
staring poppy for its morphine essence
and when that's fixed tops it all up
with soundtrack, a fatuous snatch of blackbird?

Offset his pleasure that day after waterlogged day
hangs me on the wrench, the hope
of visitors who exhaust with kindness
(but think: spoilt compared with some;
the telly twittering its limelit lashes,
the phone on a longer, handier flex,

the room draught-snug, scent-sprayed, warm)
to whom I talk unstoppably, wanting to endorse
me as me still, or as a check, lest they anticipate
next year's Tyrolean holiday?

Depose his bitchery, peeping while
with grandad's gnarled shillelagh
I bang for the eunuch (snoring upstairs)
so he can bedpan me, take
a stiff arm's length away — the stench;
or if he's absent — stranded, presuming on my illness —
ring up someone I half-know
then sit there, on cancer-toffee bones
that can snap like a baby's — that easy,
in higher childishness grunting, forcing,
till freedom farts imperiously through?

Wear down his games . . . night's the worst:
do I sleep or don't I?
If I do, what dreams clamp down . . .
cruellest when running, swimming . . .
or disorientated, where am I?
In bed or on a ledge baiting
the spasmed lightning that hurtles if I move . . . ?

Yet one strength has this cocky Torquemada
irresistibly overlooked:
that double-agency whose charm about my wrist
babbles like a tap half-turned —
whom the sultan thinks helps him torture
(but who in potent fact is on his blind side) —

whose every drop transfuses, glows:
dew, plasma, pack-cells . . .
seconds quicksilvering to hours
and every hour a kiss of hands
or like a bodhisattva's coming together
in a tie of peace, a mantra for the lightning . . .
till the haemophiliac sunset's past,
the charred night flaked out like a poppy-heart,
and, wild-rosy, climbing the pebbledash,
dawn succeeds: white magic
on a letter from a friend, a job to do . . .
while the blackbird burbles on, contralto;
the eunuch writes: my poem, life.

BH

The unseemly roses bloom,
and you lie in that utility box,
the colour of your eyes censored,
your skin hard and dry —
and, where the undertaker
set and left you,
mouthlocked, beyond tears . . .
that was never stiff with anyone,
nor hard save with yourself,
nor dry in any event —
remember how you'd sweat milk
before the child
turned its head, even . . .
and as for being set
no more could stand it
than the trampolining plover
flat sky.

DOWSER'S FUNERAL

Not as you time it, but when grace wills
— the love you hadn't substance for,
the grief you'd thought rock-dry —
rushes the lank twig in your despairing hands —
and suddenly, earth's artesian to the eyelids,
tears come, blurted like shooting-stars,
spontaneous heaven in their wake;
matching the dead's cascading brilliance,
making this flared apocalyptic night
headstone for her chiselled myth,
veined marble for its telling.

WIDOWER

Holes, spaces — not just in the small of the back
where her cushioned belly used to press,
but conversationally: missing even
those niggles about smoking less.

Missing most what was taken for granted —
the greatest, subtlest part, behind the eyes;
chasing a foam-sly figurehead without a ship,
hoping to check — the sea.

Holes, spaces, spawning themselves, endless.
That growths in her should leave such craters elsewhere! —
brutal vacuums sucking one to them
like bottles over boils, hurtful cure.

Sleepless, wanting the earthly full of her
even if varicose, unclean;
pacing, picking her ruins over
like a starved cat casing a blitzed town.

Frantic, straddling a lost smoulder
like a newspaper trying to nerve a flame;
giving up, piling the uncaught
with wet trash of regret, shame.

Holes, spaces: dragging a black tunnel,
her white shadow walking through one still . . .
the space in the mind, cold air;
the hole in the heart, irreparable.

HIGHWAYMAN

My heartbeat rides a strange bed,
the night sleepless with its hooves.
My love is in the coach ahead —
even with the rowelled stars
at heel I'll not waylay her now —
naked, at the crossroads, suiting
a colder, swifter thief.

IRREPARABLE

I wrote you when she died.

To me you were still solid:
a tartan friendship
still warm enough to wear.

For eleven salt months, no word.
Then, a Christmas card.
You wrote, it was too
inadequate to post.

I can't forgive.

Touch, not art,
was what I wanted

— an old man's scrawl,
a simpleton's cross —

touch, the bald
illiteracy of faith,
all I craved.

SURPLUS

You hoarded, all our married life.
'New things cost the earth', you'd say.
Now, I have a key without a door,
a box of nails, a tube of fixit,
two cobwebbed candles in a jam-jar,
and so much rope I could cheerfully enmesh
a time-tripped colony of dinosaur.
But of yourself, nothing.
New things cost the earth.
And you've enough of that.

PURPOSE BUILT

Stuffed, worse than living,
a pike stares
from my stagnant wall.

Until I had to,
I couldn't see it.
Now, there's
nothing else.

That eye,
that
frozen ulcer . . .

hook up:
bitten,
drowned.

A QUESTION OF TIME

Do not enquire of the sacred young
straddling a twined moment's
magnolia flesh

Or of the middle-aged, coasting
expansive years round
firelit brandy glasses

Ask the old whose bones break.

OLD WOMAN BLUES

This afternoon I wet the bed.
But I'm good mostly. Quiet, dead.

They put bars up at night,
in case I fall out, fight.

I tell them I was something once.
'Poor old Mum', they chirp, and break for lunch.

Yesterday won't travel. Only
tomorrow's the answer to me.

What can you do with old folk?
Pray they're lucky, fade like smoke.

OLD MAN BLUES

Careful faces round my cot —
think I don't know what I've got.

Drugs that kill pain.
Pain kicks them, starts again.

Sleep? Fine, when you've got the stuff.
Sit up? Grand, until you cough.

If I were only a spinster's cat
they'd drop me in five seconds flat.

One sheet's all the bed I want.
I can't make it. And they won't.

ANTICS

I'm tired and he's tired

Me, of hearing him whimper
every stick-paced step

he, of my daft talk
about getting better soon

— he tells me the pain laughs at drugs
and that he can't bend his wrist

On his birthday he goes
to a safari park

hullabaloos of monkeys
mob the car

a life crazy as his
only active

he says he hopes
to see me again

wishing no doubt
I was a monkey

SURVEILLANCE

She terrifies me, the old lady —
clomping that stagnant junk of a house.

We've to shout through the letter-box —
if she's that way in she won't answer —
just stumps around somewhere inside,
muttering, swearing

then suddenly she'll appear in the village
for bottles of tonic wine,
chuffed as a kid at the first bluebell;
smiling, trading with that cracked voice-
thirty years back if a day —
when she was governess to the squire's children . . .

Blue-spotty bread away in drawers,
pins, ribbons, a stack of bills —
the neighbours eyeing the doorstep daily
for more than one bottle of milk,
telling each other it isn't right
she should totter round with those candles —
three storeys, she could fall down
any of them . . .

Two jumpers on, one back to front,
the kettle boiled dry, its black rump out,
soot on the forehead, sticks in the bath,
what do I want with meals on wheels
home help and stuff like that
you're not supposed to be here
besides Sunday's a day of rest

Bunioned knuckles double-locking the door,
vexed eyes squinting at people in the courtyard —
offcomers . . . police, nurses . . .
shaking their heads at the curtained face, nodding . . .

What's she doing with her senile routines,
besotted confidence that she's all right,
and that everyone bar her nephew down in Cornwall's
a shameless interfering pokeabout?

What's she doing, not knowing what she's like,
what's she doing like this —
gritting our nerves, walking our dreams
like that matchwood nonsense of a house —
every live next day stoking
our fearful hopeless responsibility?

SUPPER

Eyes are closed but the mouth remains.

Beyond kisses, children, prayer,
that avid toothless mouth:
lengthening as she sleeps, the old woman —
pulling the skin shiny over
the bone-strut, coming
certain, unignorable.

All that was desired is done. Now,
with cares, duties, laid away,
she consummates her ultimate reduction
— engrossing, stark economy —
simple, of the mouth.

'Open your mouth and shut your eyes
to see what God will send you.'
So her mother once, with spooned jam.

She has already heard
the sibilant swift wings.
A chosen fledgling
in blind tropistic rapture
she waits, waits

the last and first parental shadow,
grub of heaven, death.

THE CRONES OF APHRODITE

1   *The Golden Bucket*

TRUE NORTH

Still. Fine, straight as a needle.
Still. Flower scent, threading the needle.
The growl of dark, sniffing, padding off.
Turn slowly, half left.
She is turning with you;
buttocks brushing yours.
Again. She is behind you.
Your eyes are open, still.
The swish of darkness, cool, away.
And you, dry with listening
(can you hear her breath behind?)
Turn back, singly, half right.
Half right again, intent, slow.
Breast to breast. Lip to lip.
The well of the female.
The golden bucket.

SEX KITTEN

The spit of her deadly mistress, cowled
with slant eyes crab-apple green,
conjured on the dusky chair
she slews her head to look at me —
stretches, yawns, her tiny tongue
like a pink petal slightly damp;
airs her teeth and claws then
half-miaouws enquiringly.

The furry ingénue, not yet
committed to her broomstick dam;
the dogeared roué, mangey sire
of riches bleaker than the sun,
ironically coupled here,
different in time, no more,
scent each other, whimper, stare —
she for what she doesn't know,
I for what I do.

THE LOVERS

It would be easier if they were on
a cinema screen; one could absorb them.
Here on this station platform
the feeling's faintly voyeuristic.
Though why is enigmatic: these
are only naked with happiness.
A dangled scarf and a pair of high heels —
they look to be seventeen, no more.
She flutters off to a sweet machine,
falls on him like a sunbeam,
feeds him chocolate neat as a bird.
He takes her into the haven of his smile,
hands on shoulders rocks her gently,
as a lazy tide a boat.
And now she's crowded into his arms again,
stippling his face with quick, light kisses.
Explosive as a Samurai sword
the northern flier slices past.
It could be a breeze, the notice it gets.
Why are they travelling? We don't know.
What they're waiting for they already have.

FOREPLAY

Even so intimately one
we're different. Time, timing.

I just want to look,
hang glide above the tarns of your eyes;
hold your face as it is
in the proud unspillable grail of my hands;
some incredible inch I haven't touched,
touch again.

You don't love like that:
opaque to such fine dalliance
want your joy savage:
the frantic mainline drug
with its blind explosive piston.

Don't rush me.
Anticipation can close the eyes;
but death, too, has that privilege.

INDEPENDENCE DAY

You're trying to tell someone you love them —
to cast love
into a simple shape:
a gift of tulips, straight-backed, incisive;
but the door bangs, your aunt's due
at five fifteen, there's dogs to feed
(and maybe she doesn't like tulips, anyway) . . .
always the act of reverence upstaged,
the unborn word miscarried, desire
gatecrashed by rabble circumstance
— steamy overcoats, rosettes, rattles —
a football crowd in a foyer, jamming
any private eloquence, choking
till the feast's sick as a wired buttonhole;
faceless, soon scuffed beneath.

But think: was it possible anyhow,
that fine apocalyptic oath?
Even with props right: the rostrum free,
kiss reciprocal, that wizard stone
window-dressed, decided on —
would it have clinched, each priceless syllable
an absolute, convinced, clear?

Can one ever say it perfectly, isn't
the self-contained its own taboo,
the set jewel death?

GYNAE WARD

Pasts may have dodgy memories;
futures X ray eyes.

The day's blue for a boy, pink or grey.
One in five's a miss, the figures say.

Scrapes, caesareans, hysterectomies —
up and down the lift sighs.

Sometimes it's folks: get tarted up
for scraps of home, bootee-gossip.

Sometimes a sheaf of women's mags,
bland as syrup of figs.

Sometimes marooned on soiled beds,
pain's vice jamming the eyelids

Sometimes pride in grief unspoken,
the first outraged sob not taken

till the bulkhead's split wide,
the heartless waste away on the tide.

LEAPFROG

He was at his probing climax when the knock came.
Finger to lip she motioned silence.
The knock came again, brusque, staccato.
A paused infinity of heartbeats then
something half-pushed through the letter box.
She wrenched from his embrace, no, she must away
past the wedding ring left on the dressing table
to the strange note stuck there.
'Do not, but want, to know you.
Will wait again tonight'.
'Only a bill' she muttered, climbing back.
But at their cold gyrations each knew it:
that slam of a letter box on his heart
would crack her into action like a starter's gun.
Who slips a ring vaselines a lover.
She'd be there as invited, whatever place.
Curiosity, a brisker sauce than lust,
would see her loose again,
and him, out.

BRUSHOFF

He'd stopped at the phone box, just to say he'd be late —
and, artless as the day the affair started,
walked into its blazing cenotaph.
Torn dance stubs, scuffed matches, beercan rings,
the floor was hell-deep, rotten with them.
Her dialled faces spun before him;
stuck at one, some one else's, clenched, final.
Words of fire, that searing sentence
from a cold flame, stunned his burning ear.
The carrion of desire, broken necked,
was still swinging from its gallows flex
when he walked out of it, rain began:
the random pissing of a drunk, oblivious.

CANINE INTERLUDE

a kid's dirty story
about getting stuck

a marriage parable

somehow that couple on the road
had made it in reverse, the dogs —

ending up how one wouldn't have thought
possible, rump to rump

but there it was: shunted buttocks,
a slewed yelping tandem,
mortise-fast

who trapped who
didn't want to let go

or was it a structure-catch
not found till felt

anyway, they weren't
getting out of it,
out of each other

but no one had power any more,
only bewilderment, fear

so neither minded interference
— to be straddled
like fleece-heavy sheep —
then prised apart

he licking a bloodshot arthritic finger,
she a sloppy gaping hurt —

both on their
collarless, private ways . . .

And would there be seed?

EYE OF THE IGUANA

They were here on their honeymoon; her little finger
looping his like the tail of a sea-horse.
They have come from where they started, twenty years ago —
same room, same seafront hotel. Only
the small black car outside extra.
The rose he'd given her that afternoon
stands between mirrors, memorial, opulent;
the wine on the dresser, vintage assured,
looks sleekly at them, potent still.
Then why does she say 'Darling, we're both tired'
and drop off in her dressing gown —
halfway through his answer.
Why does he stare, head in plaited hands,
at the monstrous, indifferent ceiling —
remembering how in the zoo that afternoon
he'd watched the iguana, its glass desert . . .
till the moment he sensed it looking at him —
not even outside.

STOPOVER JUNCTION

Items on the bed: one secretary bird,
one spectacled cobra, tycoon size.
Items on the floor: pyjama legs,
a flounce of nightie, two scoops of bra.
The pillows wild with stray hairs —
some dyed, some natural (grey).
One's stuck to a fang, like a kipper bone;
he takes it out, spits to make sure.
Elegant bum, oozy loins, they doze, deliquesce.
Soon he's in sleep's basket,
taken over by Bengali flutes;
while she snores up oily sheikhs
writhingly submissive to a stamped foot.
At four she wakes. Should she cold-cream her face?
No. She has decided it's love,
looks snakily at him, tells him so.
Eyes swimming, loins topped up,
he salivates assent.
She eats him out of his scaly cheque book,
into tomorrow's wifely arms.

MACHO

So many conquests, clipped and filed
compulsively, like old coins;
so many guests, explored and left —
swords of longing in their loins.

In every drawer some piece he'd made
notoriously his own;
on every wall a scabbard wailing
wetly for its overtone.

So many little deaths, until
the greatest flashed him its riposte;
no longer haunted, he could stay
irrevocably, grandly, lost:

tenant of a dark motel
impervious to their stale surprise:
the crones of Aphrodite, creaming
magic from his monstrous thighs.

JACOB AT FIFTY

A tyrant, curmudgeonly,
that broke my youth, for seven squalid years
bound me to hatred in a grinning field.
And now, he offers me his instrument —
blandly, from the wilderness,
that long armed autocrat the staff!

A last pointer! As of old, Laban;
punctual in irony as ever in deceit.
But here, I take it: committed, kiss
the wrinkled runes, that of their cunning sway
these blind fingers to what's absolute!

She was the ugly sister. By a hidden law
you thrust her on me like a headstall.
Dreadfully I matched her maidenhead,
drastic, spiked her chastity
spilling, in revenge's rancid hope,
blood that hurt you as your own

pulsing, as the frantic act progressed,
by compensation with a sister at the well;
for whom I'd shouldered back the stone of time
and known as nights of longing in my palms:
a psalm of nippled wishes burning
to the rigid rightness of my bed.

That night's beyond; with it many stars.
I stood its rigours to discover — what?
Once the alien's encountered from within
she gushes to the shaft as to a dowsing rod,
the shabby mosses of her sufferance
anointed, wonderful, enduring to the need . . .

while that exploiting the approved conceit
of catkin fingers and magnetic hips
lock, writhe, petition as it will
can never, no, until the flesh is old
and God's great pity shoaling ravenously through
hold, inviolably mould
the deeper covenant, the body of the seed.

Master, my hand upon your gift —
with it, warmth for a veteran percipience.
This wand of ancestry has more than us, it seems.
Universals make its furrowing, its grain.
And dark daughters, that have earth about them, root
more fruitfully than blonde familiars in the air!

2   *Smells Like A War*

NEVER SUCH A GAME

Noughts and crosses, noughts and crosses,
you and the kids played it everywhere:
between outraged columns of Sunday papers,
cut into lumps of soap, in sandpit lairs,

over chalked blackboards between bells,
on hopscotched pavements
and summer walls,
noughts and crosses came into it all.

Nought was a child's mouth slack with wonder,
gawping at high-wire aerobats;
cross was the look on Granny's face
when you drank out of a sloppy saucer.

Nought was something you spelt like nougat,
only not so nice;
cross was the right you knocked Dempsey down with,
only twice as great.

Noughts were spinning, prancing tops,
noughts were your wishes in millions;
crosses barbed wire rips in your pants,
unexpected, countable kisses on cards.

Never such a game for catching on;
every pushing, jealous mother's son,
every cocky shaver, wanting in —
till the fun was yours no longer —

till nought was steel rims smelling of cordite,
crosses something that proved their aim;
life remaining a hole in the heart;
nobody won, could win, that game.

FOR MY FATHER

A brace of medals my mother cursed
— 'great heavy things like that banged through the letter-box';
a pre-France diary bald as a shopping list
— 'C.O's Inspection. Played snooker';
a couple of pencil sketches, one of an old lady
in a black bonnet, leering like Nellie Wallace —
the other, ('Geoffrey coming to meet his Dad') —
an urchin dragging a tin can on a string
all that I have of you that got me,
who only knew me on your last leave:
something tender caught between seething troopships,
a soft boulder in a spilling womb.
That, and a sun-bilious snap —
you in shorts and puttees, taken
before you stood to your other bed
in that white, Salonikan cemetery.

Testimonial or dossier, I've tried to map you:
what's me in you, what couldn't be.
Your nose is mine. Some sooty moods.
You kept a pet banjo; I dribble jokes.
You took mice to church; I tease the kids.
You wanted me circumcised. Once, I was Christ's child.

Too stooped and few, your friends couldn't help.
Not even our women folk — those compulsive totters-up
of worth and foible — said anything much.
It was all so teasing — insultingly vague.
From what was mostly said, you rate as ordinary.

FOR MY FATHER (2)

But what did your Army pals make of you?
Were you so carefully nondescript all that time?
Did you never fart on parade, buck the R.S.M.,
bone tar-bright boots on a glasshouse bed?
Laugh at Lille whores sucking francs up their twats?
Bayonet, boast about it?
Somewhere, in that stew of mud and limbs,
did you chance the Spandau's crossfire, bring someone in?

One thing I needn't check —
that between the whimper of shells
and that sick headache of a helmet,
you thought of me.
And that once I had a death dream:
Nellie Wallace, her eyes out like chisels,
fixing me from the newel in the hall.

If you'd stayed, how would we have made out?
Would we have scrabbled for my mother, lost each other
in brothers and sisters, hated more than most?
Or could we have lived in and out of each other,
would it have lasted, worked?

So many frayed, irresolvable questions
nagging the static void.
Meanwhile, we can still meet —
that slapstick urchin trailing his tin can
comes through it all . . .
your small, indispensable talent
I could sometime maybe have capped, saluted
in words as native, funny.

SONG OF THE AIRBORNE WIDOW

O my love had a cap of purest cherry,
a salute tall as a poplar tip,
a belt and smock of forest green,
a flying horse at his shoulder.

He swung the sky like a bough down to me,
held me, catapulted back;
we drifted all a summer's heaven
like blossom on the trees of May.

One day he left to cross the water —
before his luck could open out
took his falling last of sun
glinted from the barrel of a gun.

Now he lies on a strange common,
bullets buttoning his smock;
his canopy a silken wreck,
his cap hung on a rifle butt.

Stop his watch on its last heartbeat,
twist his ring till the knuckle bleeds;
put away his weekly letters
till his unborn son can read.

A cap, a cup of darkest cherry.
O love, when you were flaunting
I came to give you life, not lead —
but it was death that you were courting.

HOME OF THE BRAVE

The last rocket thumps and hisses,
spills its avalanche of stars.
They'll be lighting the great bonfire now.
We duck the ropes, through to the reservation
where its sacrificial tipi stands.
Already, fire-bitten kids are round;
whooping it up like braves, white hot.
Two drag another by his shouting arms
— a slice of gut where the shirt pulls up —
then seconds off the scalping heat
leave him slumped: a blur of old skins.
Is he hurt or shamming? Tribal victim
or tender, cherished fool? We can't see from here.
Firemen stand by, a casual clan.
Poles crack, a tyre stinks — something is falling;
somewhere a cross; burning, falling.

SEMBLANCE

'What looks like, the outward appearance of, something' O.E.D.

The street could have seen you through the curtains, it seems —
only it didn't. Nor the broody bluebottle rasping by.
But you'd been there, on the floor of that hot, shut room
a flat month before police broke in —
time enough for colonial maggots to share, it seems.
A box came, not overbig. Sweating, swearing,
somehow they muddled you in. Your head was black, split rock;
what was clothing might have been flesh.
Someone who thought she remembered you by sight called in.
They gave her a blue gauze cap and powdered gloves.
'Could be anyone. Smells like a war' she said.
They wanted to do it from the teeth; you had no dentist.
Nor any kin, to judge from papers left.
Only cacti. Vultures would have been kinder,
but it was cacti: rows of them, bleached, spiny,
on sills, shelves, everywhere.
How did you come here? What did you do? Who were you?

TO A WARTIME PRO

It's different, all Civvy Street now —
the roads that saw the trooping of your colours
verboten, underground;
the hotel porticos where you Venus flytrapped
your swilling punters athletic cards in windows.

I miss it somehow: the flagrant flower clock
of Piccadilly where you had your time;
and Eros in a tidfer or Yankee brown
— with eyes more suited to the sights of a .22 —
stormed that douche-spattered polyglot knoll of a Mons Pubis.

Still, that kohl and ketchup hello of a face
must have liberated more
than the odd testis;
those battle honoured, fetching scars
(implied but factual) turned somebody on.

And though you snapped your castanets of heels
cockily enough at prudes and cops,
manned with uncertainty, arm in arm
with the dubious and desperate
you surely walked, like us.

Maybe in that drastic line even more so:
a guerrilla wounded in the naked war on love,
a sniper picking off more than you could lose.
So, I salute you. Forgive if it's only a hand —
hardly your principal organ of concern, if I remember.

STANDING ORDERS: HAMBURG

Sodium shadows, oneway signposts
with hips jutting, shoulder bags,
grounding heels terse as rifle butts
the whores muster, move off.

Posted to rancid coverts
for short arm practice;
dropped at bedsit arsenals
to dogwhip sin;

into the wrangling wallet,
the pimp's muscle,
the gonoccocal ambush,
the time bomb of the spirochaete,

oldest of contemptibles,
newest of dupes,
committed, casual, brief,
the whores rally, bash on.

FUN BEACH

The inflatable elephant rears its trunk,
a colic of kids in its bouncy belly.
Longs to flop, envies the skunk.
Round the mini track, in endless rally
— mod, rocker, skinhead, punk —
zap the broncho boys, the Yamaha ceilidh.

Slurp, backwash. Assorted gobs
cruise the fruit machinery, slotting in.
The mike-hooked bingo barker ad libs,
blue tracer spurts from the star gun;
the laughing clown parades his shattered ribs,
the sharpshooter his bull's-eye Zen.

Outside, bathed in each other's eyes,
oblivious to gulls and golfball shrapnel,
Adam the archetypal fall guy
and Eve with her briny snaketail hair
are plaiting adorable, sun-oiled thighs
into a promise of lollies and cot-banged yells

while with pipes and knitting stretched along the quay
the not quite dead assume a peace,
eyes on salvationist hills above the bay
where sweptwing tomahawks, practised, tireless,
are opening up the blues of sky
like children's heads: spare, anonymous.

3 *The Slow Conveyor Belt*

SUNDAY CANAL

The slow conveyor-belt goes on.
Inverted workers perch on clouds.
Floats drift, are checked, re-sited,
maggots nailed and slung.
The slow conveyor-belt goes on,
seraphic cloud-heads, sitting ducks,
targets, nooses in its flow . . .
the slow conveyor-belt goes on,
the truce the black messiah gave,
the dream-shift, by grasping Monday
unhooked, thrown back alive.

SHROPSHIRE UNION

On fingers sure as a wine waiter's
old Telford's aqueduct takes the air,
comes to earth again calm as a canal,
swerves left at the marina then in a sepia dream
towards Sunday moorings at Llangollen.
On, into its endless slide
go pleasure boats: T shirted deckhands straddling
bowsprit Union Jacks; captains in shorts judging
the points of a tiller; wives at novels;
kids climbing over (watched
with panting anticipation by assorted dogs).
The ripple-plumaged bird of the wake
— slow magic — sets off thistledown,
finds lollopy banks, vole noses,
capsized muttering anglers on stools;
under every arched and coming bridge
the sun is a temple dancer, tossing veils.
On, into its gleam, they go —
warty fenders, toy lifebelts —
under the raised eyebrows of more bridges,
through dabbed reflections of clouds between leaves,
into history, its stark reverses:
there, in the Canal Museum,
originals: those that scooped, colonised . . .

bowler hatted collarless navvies
scabbed with clay, leant on resentful picks;
curtain bonneted boat women clumped
by moleskinned pipe smoking men —
and kids who couldn't read a word that wasn't water,
trudging horses, or castled roses —
with the narrow boats that came out of it all:
the gaudy immaculate water houses
sunk to an inch above the freeboard with coal or tar
— all staring, as once
at the hooded alien photographer who caught them —
only with irony now at these pitiful upstarts:
palefaced, fancyrich comedians
daring to squat here, outlive them

LUDLOW CASTLE

The kiosk girl twists me a cornet flambeau,
the gun from Sebastopol (how did they get it here?)
cranes like a blind dog at yesterday —
and past a sentry box where one in fifty buys a guide,
over a sward of sprawled, skylarking trippers
— aunts with shoes off, kids wrestling their dads —
I walk to the restored, outrageous keep.

Thistle halberds saluting let me pass,
but my walled flesh is ragged with it all.
Hawkbit falls out of the creviced eye
like a shot archer held on by the toes;
a fern stuck in my throat's well
is the tongue of a hanged woman;
up there may be the courtly dove
at her languorous appeasing madrigal
but here it's feathers, droppings,
every web-caught angle of bone.

TRAFALGAR SQUARE

The showgirl fountains:
ostrich plumy, glittering
flesh tints, champagne skirts.

The old charwoman,
away from such vanity —
even so, spray touched.

Typhoon of pigeons,
braking for lenses, manna,
sunlit shoelace tips.

A drunk, crossing late,
in a wild concertina
of foghorns, sirens.

Again the pigeons.
One on a boy's head. Behold:
Big Chief Sitting Bird!

Watery banners
slipped from the hands of children.
Fountains lost at sea.

WATERLOO BRIDGE

Between the last stone, the formal consecration,
Valkyrian they set their flying face —
a race of swans, in constellation bearing
out of time's thunderheads miraculous down.

To their fall as if snow-shared the river gave.
Where they slept — like tents on melting wounds —
their dream torsos impossibly hung,
their polar deference amazed.

Deception. From that night's warm hold
slipped columns, beaks of dawn;
from that turncoat flood a salt light,
an embattled, hissing chastity outshone.

They stretched, they would have gone —
then, distantly between,
hint of a drowned city's foundlings
held on the upstroke, their wings.

FROM CASTLETON THROUGH THE WINNATTS

Nothing about the vaunted caves impresses —
not their fog-yellow, snotty stalactites
nor bollard-stubby stalagmites;
neither fossil cenotaphs nor seams of blackish blue john.
But out, rid of the slimy warren,
with thistledown idling upwards
and grass that's gentle underfoot
the blessed soft rock seems natural;
its scalloped crags, minarets and pinnacles
an architecture of deliverance spurning
with white magic the catacombs it skirts.
While round the bluff and scoop of Mam Tor,
with mayfly bodies and huge triangular sails,
a mini regatta of hang gliders
takes up its thermal adagio dance;
floats, flaunts, with such euphoric ease
the eye itself decides to holiday,
dally, curtsey with them.

HIGH WIRE

Watching that steel wisp of gossamer tremble
at your first pointed irrevocable step,
what do we, what can we, expect?
Burlesque of an early flying machine
waggling its wobbly pole of wings?
Some black mutant widow of science
careering from the roof?
Neither. What's there is art:
fine-drawn essence, body, pride,
moved serious on a witty thread.

Childhood shouting from a fallen bole
'Watch me, ME!' you have saluted, passed.
Tradition, the act your father choked on
— landed wrongly, a netted fish —
you live to practise: that abysmal sliding
foot by foot over the breathless air,
the ringside slop of faces . . .
where there is only you, the end in your eyes,
treading the black grapes of our terror
into triumphant high bouquets.

BRANDS HATCH WIDOW

O he's gone, my flagrant flier,
my gusty comet, thunder revver.
The flair's gone, the wind's bright feather
and the last flag down — forever.

Gone, gone, my flamboyant neighbour,
my steel gazelle, saint in leather.
The prayer's gone and the breakneck saviour:
lightning struck by lightning's cleaver.

Singe of blood on the white clover.
The void cries, the robbed plover.
It's mourning now, that cold fever —
and the hearse, the endless river.

The arrow's snapped, the life quiver.
Man for man and wives to suffer.
O wind, fire, my rakish lover;
tyres, tears, the heart's run over.

TIDES

implore the moon
with buckets of children's fingers

scoop graves quicker than castles
empires of strutting flags

live with crab's eyes and sucked shells
scarfed weed and knotted condoms

leave their fidgety stale
in rock pools inhale their vomit

never can quite decide
where to set their frayed limits

never can stop the massive thudding clock
they set with such shifting hands of water

4   *Bury me Anywhere*

PASSION FLOWER

Slattern in hair curlers,
your apprehensive leaf-hands
everywhere;

tigress, trellis-roamer
caught in a jungle
of savage prayer;

bud of a child unborn
leant on speechless
months of air

how you get it all
— anxiety, tension, patience —
the works, the astonishing art-process

never to be hustled, tamed, induced;
that hangs incredibly
on the sun's move:

touched by that royal laser
wakes to fire only
a starfish parasol

nothing but the heart.

GALE

Raspberry canes are pooled flamingos.
A silver birch squirms like a limbo dancer.
Somebody's nicked the sky's spigot.
Somebody's mugging the last roses.

Rain's a crossfire, swirled battalions.
Wind bustles the cypress, water's up
from a punctured main, undercuts the teazle
whose busbys stagger, grenadiers in a trap.

Leaves pitch out of trees like snipers.
Brown as a ratpack, a runaway nag,
the foam slavered beck belts on.
The moon's mothballs, they've water cannoned the sun.

Useless to batter the slumped barometer.
All one can do is watch, wonder.
This mad dog with its aniseed rag
will quit when it likes, no sooner.

LAWN MOWING

The old pusher's sharp today —
purrs, oiled with sweetness;
a blur of stalks light as sawdust
whirling into, swamping its scoop.

I pour a green snowman on the air;
bits of him won't set, but dripglint —
he has a coat of fireflies, melts
in his own creation.

SWEET PEAS

They take the air
like the tossed silk
handkerchiefs
a conjuror finds
in our amazed pockets

and longer than rockets
stay with us;
the shafts of their illumination
tall, pure
as childhood.

They take the air
in sea shell colours.
Look, hear the oracle:
the wizard and his prisms gone
to saltwhite miracle.

THE VIRTUE OF SLOVENLINESS

We had an old door
roofing
the coal bunker,
but it rotted,
weather-bust.

So now
there's only
a concrete rectangle,
black scree,
and in an odd crack
the dandelion.

Every spring
(and more)
it flowers;
every winter
snaps . . .
(runaway chunks,
seismic slides,
whatever).

It's been
a corky wart
two months now,
but today I see
it's cheeky as always —
inching out
into sallow,
mucky leaf.

And that white, carrotlike root
will be somewhere underneath, probing —
the fat, inner-tubey stalk
flashing its cocky, common head . . .

Now if I was one of those fixit guys,
mail-order segments fitting together
in a dapper, blueprint dream —

insulated, waterproofed,
with a flap door craftily inserted,
and the coal only so far to the door . . .

it couldn't have lived.
Nor I.

DROUGHT

Smug as a fried egg on Wedgwood
the sun smirks its heavenly sideboard.
Soil snubs the fingers, thin as smoke;
clods turn up useless, dry as coke.

Dog-day-tongued, shanked in dust,
their sap atomised, their mettle rust,
shrubs pant for a handsome miracle
to rebaptise them, sink this pumice hell.

And what they dream is thunderheads toppling,
arrows of mercy hissing —
an after air cool as silk,
a land bathed in oases, drunk with asses' milk.

A CHRYSANTHEMUM NAMED CARDINAL

They tossed you in a dustbin to choke on thirst.
Though you were flawless: fire and bronze,
delicate as a sea anemone.

The rest we'd saved — those blonde bubblecuts —
charred in a fortnight. You stayed:
a cool immaculate smoulder, quite intact.

Till it seemed even you must wither —
your petals turn to raddled claws
then sag, a mophead tangle.

Dying back to that fiery centre
I smelt your essence: a bronze bouquet;
earth and air, indestructible.

GRASS

She asks are flowers alive, do they know each other.
I teach her to taste the grass.
Tiny white moths blur the path,
jackknife to stalks, slip the igloos of our hands.
I teach her to draw out the lighter part
wonderful as a sword, taste it.
She brings harebells a shade darker than mine,
a spider's tightrope stretched from the flower of one.
I teach her to dunk the blade in subtle spit,
tongue, switch it from cheek to cheek.
She picks a plume with seeds like moths asleep,
sticks it in brilliant teeth, says 'Look, it's fainted!'
   – tells me the taste's gone, that she's drinking rain.

JARDINS SOUS LA PLUIE

Young, I used to watch and wonder
at the old men who haunted front room windows –
what was there to look at, why couldn't they find
something else, vital, in the house?

Yet, to be still, to see movement itself holy
– by the striped and crinkled basket of a tulip
a pansy's sudden geisha face –
is oneself assuredly to move.

What the gnarled saints in their cathedral cliff
have always seen, I see now:
rain snapping its thousand eyelids,
the slanted resurrection of a world.

RAIN

The great pine of the world is sifting
its endless needles.
I drink to sibilance, the stealthy fall.
The silver birch has fresh buds,
each catkin its crystal word.
From hook to bough in the sky's window
the washing line waits like a rope of pearls
for consummation, lover's flesh.
The stream is filling up.
A thrush sings. Bury me anywhere.

SALT, ROSES, VINEGAR

FRONTIERS

One was a gate, open.
Behind, a baby in a pram,
screeching for a dropped rattle.
Was it booby-trapped? He went on.

Two, a door in a wall.
Holsters flanked it, smiling.
Below, splayed and dried like frogs,
some few dead.

Three had a glass booth,
a strapped-in DJ,
and his mother on tape, singing
Come home, Johnny, I'm cold.

Four, he couldn't get through to anyone.
Men were rocking the car in front,
men in the car behind bawling
Your brother's back there. Take over!

Five, it might have been Christmas Day.
A junkyard stared:
bricks, banners, vizors,
congealed oaths, water cannon.

Six, incredibly, was a hillside path.
Sheepdogs circled, fawned him on.
The air was curlews, tambourines,
the sun loving; naked, strong.

Different, dangerous. He left.

SCAPEGOAT

A day of flagrant trespass, breaking and entering —
him stood there not like the gaffer of legend,
smelling of rum and reindeer, choleric charity,
but workaday, dirty as a sweep. And, incredibly,
blowing it — the dark calendar, the sky's wicked chimney —
simply as his nose. And the black hurt of all the world
blasted from crevices, falling, falling
to the world's hearth, and him above it,
grinning like snow, bits of shriven soot
stippling his lightened shoulders,
god of the avalanche, snow.

SPRINGBOARD

What she dies into
this dab-flushed crone

sucking her dentures
trudging like sticks
in a cribbage board

is not her
but the white prodigious
wand of her achievement

that once,
oiled with the thrill of discipline,
catapulted from vibrant boards

the air shaped
to her singing flesh
the green element
rising to her

loving its wound

hissed and healed
between fingertips
and spliced soles

I see her shadow swirling up,
the head shake eager as a dog's,
the prowed breaststroke returning

and on her shoulder,
waterdrops

as once when glory in her
came spilling over the holy sheet,
she felt the naked, blessed tears
of the young man above her.

THINGS

The tin bath once brimmed with daughters,
the dislocated axehelve, and the trunk
of the plum-tree that wouldn't burn —
it's all there, by the disused shed
whose rivets shove out like mushrooms,
whose chipped stones are web-hoary
-moult of some random, longhaired cat.
We could have it moved, all of it. But won't.
Ruin has its own mana,
the seasoned credit of the personal.
We'll be neat as nothing soon enough —
but no-one's tipping the dustman yet.

EPICENTRES

I see no longer with a child's eyes,
only through winter's bones.
In the Garden Of Delights beyond my window
that red, bucking broncho of a bouncer
— Banbury Cross via the sunpoised greenhouse —
looms frozen, out of chapped grass:
an unreachable, taunting planet;
the slide their squeals accelerated
chutes precipitous to seams of hell;
the knot swinging from the treehouse rope
is a thirdworld orphan's shrunken head.

And what's to happen in the wilful horoscope,
the goats and scorpions of scenarios to come?
Will some freak mercy, alien gift,
harness the raw planet, mine the glaring shaft,
undo that hungry knot?

Or will headlines take care of it all —
and the children, those who can still read?

A TIMELY SURGERY

Meeting a new body, trying love again,
watch for the stitched wound, the white scorpion
with the cocked, venomous tail removed.
If you can, match it.

For here's the dispossession-sign,
the cicatrice of tribal strength
— all that rank, idealist gangrene,
dirty appendices to a frantic text,
knife-bled, come richly clean.

And this, in the play of new flesh,
is what the old tightlipped scar says:
it's over now, the spastic pain,
the heart shrilling to itself in a phone box,
the suicidal fever and the threat.

The wound's healed. The wound points
simply, to the loin.

SON

An old woman lumped on a commode,
her dognosed, punctured breasts awry —
or shuffling, fearful, the hands in mine
shuddering like mauled birds —
an old woman with nails blotched
and lips champing soundlessly...
my mother.

Like some driftwood toy obscurely scavenged
by a desperate uncalled for child,
dressed up with all the gross expensive
longing that's a poor child's,
she lingers, the lesion's puppet —
her doubled body an open question
monstrous, hard as a hook.

Rubble, I watch, praying
helplessly for some voodoo sleight,
some eyeball snarling sympathetic mask
whose apport shall blast out such devilry;
watch, all the time the chairbound
reason staring wooden at its fantasy,
the rank wish that leaves her savagely incurable.

And then, from the womb curled centre of the mystery,
asking me for something, knowing it will come,
in tones weak with tenderness, a bird's
miraculously lifting from the tongue,
her voice.

And there is no question, there was never any doubt
for me, her striding seed,
or the woman blitzed into glory at my side,
my blood's anointed, mother.

NO ANSWER

I sent flowers. They must have died in cellophane; untouched, dry.
I rang, rang. The phone buzzed me back: a capsized, stuck bluefly.
I telegraphed. The boy came back with all he'd found: a bent key.
I knocked, like thunder. My doorstep tears pawed under, sniffed the floor.
I rapped, pounded, shoved notes through, heard a dog howl, paper torn.
I sent word from the hospital, from a gut gritty with carbrital, grey.
I sent food, wedding photos, a child's toy, a rosary.
But she turned her back the length of the world . . . a year, a day.

IN THE PINES

A hare with its sandy russet
rocking horse lope comes softly in.

A brown tree-slipping shadow of an owl
drops to feathery leafmould, sleep.

The rope-spinning wind's lasso
of wild bees sounds suddenly off.

On my wrist that ladybird set
in the sun's bracelet has gone.

SALT, ROSES, VINEGAR

Battered fragments dry as loofahs,
chipped fingers, sausageskin.
The queue angles slowly supperwards,
conveyor belted, dumb.
A drunk I went to school with
stares through me, then the same again;
his eyes rancid sumps.
A girl whose mother once pulled my hair
dreams her petal cheek on cool chrome...
into its glazed, metallic finish.
A woman whose man I sacked
slants her face, starches a sidelong eye,
sets the mirror gazing at me.
The tiny blue earrings of the server
flick on and off, her left hand
scoops, wraps, scoops, wraps
it all up: dead headlines.

CAIN

On my hands the blood red as apples.
Apples always: he was stoned on cider
the night he got me, drooling home
to spit the blind pips of his manhood up
that crying rib who'd once beguiled
gold skinned and ripe as an autumnal sun.

So, I grew like it,
like an apple tree —
earth-stooped, saturnine;
my droppings windfall for the wasp,
the testy late September diehard
stinging at a look.

When I walked, the clouds slouched.
Where he did, my fair sibling
(whom both, for once, adored)
the sky danced into scarves of cirrus
— airy, deft hosannas...
for me sour as a thistle's spending.

Fruit of mine he'd never touch,
that gay stripling. Was I not infidel?
The clod with the dirty nails, the mush eater?
So, I slew him, the sheep eyed upstart,
trying to prune the bent bough,
slew him, that stole my sap.

On my hands the blood red as apples,
on my brow the red mark
where clenched resentful thighs first bruised,
undid me into bad breath . . .
to love stupidly, slay fruitlessly,
wander east of friendship, scavenge in the dust.

And no one but myself to kill me, tread
into treeless heaven this stony core.

DEATH OF A GAMBLER

The dice that thrilled
like flamenco castanets
turns up its eyed black.

His whore a screaming also-ran,
his house a toppled stack of chips,
he's gone, the natty scarecrow
with the top hat and armpit derringer.

The rosy vase
has spilt its blood.
Dust falls on the coffin
like ash from his last cigar.

PERCEPTS WITHOUT DEFERENCE

AUTHOR'S NOTE

For those new to Welsh verse forms the poems included here use some of the twenty four bardic metres codified in the 14th century. They are, however, not translations. The Twenty Englynion take as their unit the Englyn Unodi Union: a quatrain whose syllabic line count is 10, 6, 7, 7. it has one rhyme — at the line ending in the last three lines but in the first on the 7th, 8th, or — exceptionally — 9th syllable.
'Sleep Charm' Is an Englyn Proest Cadwynog, involving a 7 syllable line. 1 and 3 rhyme, 2 and 4 off-rhyme with 1 and 3. The word 'cadwyn' means 'chain'.
'Lament' and 'Poet' are rhupunts: 4 syllable quatrains whose first three lines rhyme with each other, whose last line chimes with its equivalent in other stanzas.
'Garden Cwydd' and 'Llatai Poem' employ 'cwydd': 7 syllable couplets rhyming stressed with unstressed endings. A Llatai poem is one where a lover sends a bird or animal as a messenger to his beloved.

TWENTY ENGLYNION

Dipper

A snowball, chucked downriver by a kid,
that somehow has the sly
wit to make it, even fly . . .
Or, is it all my daft eye?

River Walk

Rain on the flickering bibs of dippers,
on my pinged brolly ribs —
flip, sketching with silver nibs
a million flash ad libs.

Torchlight Procession

Sparklers in the tall hands of ghost children
headlamps dawdle downhill.
Where they level off's a sill
of show chrysanths: golden, still.

Buzzard

Coolly headless, a ghostly eye on murder,
it swivels cobalt sky;
Its heaven angelic-sly —
devout stretched lambs in its cry.

Stars

Such calm geometry needs no compass.
Countless, precise as snow,
you touch our wafer-marrow,
coruscating here below.

Under the Hair Drier

Women mouthed like sandals with soles unstuck
clack to their classic goal:
how to flatten that fat droll
of a spouse — priapic prole!

Tabloid Journalist

He's a flea in a cancan petticoat —
in a column's thighsweat
biting to scarify, yet
bloat with her blood in secret.

Foxglove

Love's digitalis. See the startled truth —
brash, exact as a tart.
What sharpens the optic dart
feathers its venereal heart.

Mole on Barbed Wire

What did you do, that the sadistic oaf
has you sat up like this —
like a dog in martyred bliss
begging for simple justice?

Buddleia

Shot of a Red Admiral cloud-flying.
Moment and shroud: the spry
pulse of prowess winking by
its coffin, lost in a sigh.

Cloudburst

The war drums batter, the Bren guns stutter.
Boneyard mouths crack open.
Grassed-over runways listen.
Sunset gutters bleed like men.

Clockface

Sworded minutes, hours of broken arrows.
Time rounds on us: the zen
of triumphant essence then
the slow vortex . . . more often.

Heron

A bone-white silhouette survives the reeds.
Vole rings have no answer.
Luck's the only theatre —
stoop, gaff, the throat of laughter.

Gander

Neck stiff as a pole, zipfastener teeth —
off my land, you town jerk,
or your calf will do for starters,
and that lush bum as a perk!

Frost Piece

Sun snipes from leaves, on stopped windscreen wipers.
Old sailors reach for rye.
Kids skate, mufflered to the eyes.
Vapour trails take days to die.

Guy Fawkes Night

He looks up, his eyes flowering rockets.
That memory's the crock
at the rainbow's foot; he'll mock
death with its star-sheaved shock.

Cloud With Stars

It sits up there like an astonished child:
the sky a tank of fish
woken at its secret wish.
Till sleep swims by; they vanish.

Child Prodigy

Dream-climbing to his treehouse piano
a star-plucked escapee
adds to their brilliance three
toccatas of Scarlatti.

Avalon

Apple tree shadow leans to pave the grass.
The sun no longer raves.
Escape has the greenest caves.
What anaesthesises, saves.

September

A leaf of Spanish chestnut fidgets free,
canoes its last rapids.
Summer's a myth, invalid —
distant as caryatids.

LAMENT

Sad runes persist.
The rain's black fist,
Its windy wrist,
strikes hard and chill.

My veins dismay,
my bones delay,
my hair drops grey
as a goosequill.

Bleak shadows baulk.
the air is hawks;
the spider talks.
I sign my will.

What stifles spring,
that bright changeling?
Does winter bring
Its gallows-cart?

No favour's worn,
no child Is born;
the poignant thorn
commands my heart.

No wide-eyed dawn,
no unicorn;
the raindropped thorn
my pregnant art.

POET

The word is here,
the mission clear
Its quarry near —
I know my way:

quest of the sky,
its lyric eye
mine to deny
the stolid tree.

The door is there,
the spiral stair,
the waiting chair —
I have the key.

My song the quest,
Its will the test,
I stride possessed —
decisive, free.

In my hand shells,
on my lips spells;
against truth's wells
I hold the sea.

SLEEP CHARM

Twilight river, lazy prow,
take me down your reaches, slow;
tie me up beneath the bough,
tap my senses, limpid, low.

Pelt of vole, wand of willow,
drift of swan, wing of swallow,
cool my brow, fan my pillow,
bring me where none shall follow.

Harebell's deft marimba chime
deepen eyelids, loosen limbs;
bud of poppy, heartleaf lime,
slough the body and its whims.

Plume of bulrush, flower of thyme,
curl me to your water-womb;
hold me spellbound in a rhyme,
seal its analeptic tomb.

GNOMIC STANZAS

Clouds piling, the moon's delight —
stream-jumping like a child's kite.
The fair man's fortune is light.

Clouds piling, with a jet's far
smoke trail white-neat as a spar.
Whose past is straight needs no star.

Clouds piling, a sunset mess
whose aim is a shadow's guess.
On the last peak one's headless.

GARDEN CYWYDD

Welsh poppies soft-crinkly stood;
Greek helmets miscalled monkshood;

Musky pink's areola;
Sweet William's lapped-over star;

Mites tiptoeing moschatel;
bees in the foxglove's tunnel;

Sunsleek blackcurrant berries:
green grappling-irons (sweet peas);

Snapdragon in fine cocked hats;
spun-gossamer lariats:

Percepts without deference —
their certain alibi, sense.

LLATAI POEM

North of Kendal, the Kent's flow,
forktailed amazing swallow
swift as a crossbow quarrel
go from Staveley to Stock Ghyll —
to Trish, old Godsell's daughter,
my fancy, my loving spur.
Neat skimming bird, dear migrant,
go to, tell how much I pant
— virtuoso, stunt-flier
scything the astonished air —
for her breathing presence here;
who lies smooth as a river,
her weeping-willowy hair
dangled, her buttock dimpled.
Take hungry eyes, words unsaid,
to cherish her nipples' rose:
gentle hands, winged shadows,
to glide over, caress her;
a strong-loined sun, that she bear
what's future in love's present —
bold in ripeness, never want.

MY GHOST IN YOUR EYE

THRENODY

Dawn's an arthritic slut with a dishcloth,
wringing night into an iron pail.
What she'll rise to's a bitter broth —

for Anarchy's returned, worse than a Visigoth,
to sack the churches, spit in the Grail —
no pinups on its calendar of wrath —

and orange and green split the streets, beating a drum;
winds clobber the parks, strip the roses;
the writing's on the wall, the brahmins dumb.

Who shouts for housing reserves his slum.
Who cries for water's turned on by hoses.
Who asks for bread divides a crumb.

Famine's son looks from a thousand bill boards
— ribs a snatch of broken ladder,
broken by the jackboot toes of war lords.

Desolation's daughter walks on swords
— a delicate bloody-footed gadder —
to a brothel of clapped frauds.

The fountain that pranced lish as a spiracle
dries like — an actor, a kneecapped clown.
Whirlpools gulp the last coracle.

From her schizoid mount the trepanned oracle
with the barred lips stares strangely down
on graffiti: wall of no miracle.

Pesticides abort the four leaved clover.
Touting pocket lasars, skintight hoods,
treading on old shadows the new take over.

Didn't you see me flashing? Out, for the onceover.
You're a road runner now, not lapped in backwoods.
Be my cur. Sit: I'll call you Rover.

Fall-out falls in with the hi-tech marchers.
Heat's gone out of the good ghosts.
There are no arrivals. Only departures.

The saints are gone and the witty archers,
the sun-massaged and embracing hosts.
Nothing but scorpions now — and cucarachas.

History bears with the thighs of robots.
Women writhe, raped by inhuman dreams.
Babes die strangers, in their cots.

Did you think those diving planes guillemots?
Check on it. Count the screams.
Bet your dirty boots there'll be dead. Lots.

Revolution's a rag. Critics crawl.
The Saviour's a dead fish left on the shore.
The writing's on the wall, where there is a wall.

Where to go to escape the caterwauling?
When the chauffeur skeleton's there at the door,
the writing on the wall, a black sky falling?

SCORPION

Why does history equate you with the death-god?
Blaze the sky with you, a constellated warning?
Bless with your name a whip of steel spikes?

Why do we fear you — that stealth, silence —
among us so swiftly in a corner's shade,
the cocoon of a sock . . . comfortable, lethal places?

Is it that headlong look, that parade of weaponry:
the Id's empire like a Roman galley
oaring relentlessly in?

Or the horny obsession with survival —
pouncing on munchy vibes, dancing the clinched female
step by step to the spawning floor?

One of your tribe can take out a horse in minutes.
But what awes most is the immunity:
if there are stones left after the nuclear night

you and no other blood will be under them.

THE ABOMINABLE SNOWMAN

The end is clear. It would be almost simple
still to achieve it. Without glasses even
the rock shows that would conserve the cairn,
where the only future could unshakeably adore
its wind-muscled superhuman flag.

Almost. But already there are tracks;
black with empathy, definitive.
It is over. The Unspeakable has gestured;
its message grafted shambles back
still virgin-savage to its freezing lair.

And though the weather's southerly, the picks glint
with whetted confidence, the deft intact
transistor rushes wordy oxygen
to mask our weariness, inspire and save —
there is no answer, ever, ever.

Too brusquely did we beard the oracle.
Perfection, (the Unspeakable's bright master),
disdains us. No longer have we tongues
but slump apart, upon outlandish packs,
wet-sandbagged with the folly of ascent...

crestfallen, while sickeningly below
forgotten chasms crane remindingly:
crevasses of intransigent despair,
bottomless eternities that take
the dregs of yet another dream

like slack snow, irreversibly . . .
to watch it wreathing slowly downward
with obscene patience, the mad calm
of monsters that are nothing but deny
the blessing even of a last propitiation,
the part atonement of a death.

LANDSLIP TERRACE

Wouldn't you like a house on a cliff then?
take this one — look at the view, the bay
(you'll have seen it on posters coming up).
Fab, yes: that laughing girl
with the complete, inviting bosom,
those dinky yachts rounding the famous point,
streets wound quaintly to a golden beach...
and fish besides, fresh, cheap.

Look at it all, anything now you're here.
This wall edge, does it cant a trifle?
Soon righted (the usual drill
moving the piano back a foot or two).
And if the thing nags always
your job to go to: that comfortable suction
the other way... expectant chores,
a colleague's chirpy grin,
the boss commending, the old bonus due.

Reception? If at night the telly's
dodgy (atmospherics, say)
the stuffs there, snug, snazzy
— built in cabinet, bed settee —
for a nip of elsewhere, a shot of sex —
on the house, of course.
And if tomorrow's that heartbeat thinner
well there's more stuff (van comes up
Fridays, on the ringing dot).

Erosion? Bit of a drag, true —
but then there's always some gimmick to engage:
steel stakes (if not too pricey)
and anyway, driftwood for the fetching,
and marram grass, in case of a sand push.
Ask the kids what: they'll have some bright comeback —
funny too . . . calling the Keystone Cops maybe.

Tides? You're thinking of that sea perhaps,
as it lopes now, wolf-grey;
curling a closer lip, taking a toothier look
(Here's one bone the fellow fancies, that we know!).
Still, nothing yet — in spring the creature
can be frisky, quite a lamb really . . .
and anyway, there's neighbours with priority —
so one hopes.

What's that? Don't think you're quite up to it yet,
bit ambitious for one so young?
Not to worry. Time's free.
See you next year, if this lot's gone
there'll be something else as definitely YOU.
And every year the price drops, remember . . .

INTERVIEWING THE MEGABOSS

And what if you run out of solid fuel?
I'll have nuclear plants from here to Peru.
And the waste? I'll think about that
the next three thousand years or so.

And what will you do about education?
Spill a million tabloids, keep 'em dumb.
And should you run out of paper? Hire a bunch
of mutant wasps to chew me some.

And what will you do to house the people?
Put up skyscrapers, split the moon.
And when you've run out of concrete?
My boffins. Do a bomb with superglue.

And what when there's no more room on earth?
There'll be space on the airbus.
And if you run out of time? Oh, that.
Recycle it, of course.

And what if folk don't do what you say?
I take them out. It's part of the game.
And if you run out of death? Don't be childish;
I'm making it all the time.

BOW STREET RAG

O the heron necked reporters and their shorthand books,
the processed P.C's thick as rooks,
the twelve good men set up like skittles,
their bottoms numb, their thoughts on victuals . . .
muddled, saddled, sticking it to lunch

O the whisky troupers and the vodka-shot,
the sideways bedded and the misbegot,
the winkled hags and wrinkled lags,
sleep-in-their-clothesy drop outs, drags . . .
contorted, thwarted, beaten to the punch

O the fancy fiddlers and extortion crows,
shopwindow pros, flash so-and-so's,
the shysters, heisters, brothel-sheikhs,
cosh and conmen, widow-rakes . . .
alive alive-o, stewing in a bunch

O the crafty cads and unlucky lads,
onetime comics, alltime sads,
the young advocates so bland and buttery,
the court veterans, so grand and sputtery . . .
mixing, fixing, sparring for a hunch

O the upper crustys, living graciously by rules;
the lower lustys, thriving edgily on fools;
the protective bruisers and the demo queens,
the wrong foot choosers and the squashed betweens . . .
heard and hanging . . . waiting for the crunch

NIGHT BIRDS: NEWCASTLE

A cop's helmeted shadow
stops at a punk's scratched face.
The bluefly taxi clocks in, out;
whizzing round, picking up someone's pieces.
In the maithuna of shop doorways
a few couples still exist.

St.John The Baptist — a gold hand —
moves, notches ten past two.
Veiled with starlings its rawboned trees
stand silent as widows in black lace;
only to lose their sensuous grief
minutes later, when the swirled epiphany's
a mob again, gracing
the spattered stones of Central.

There are pigeons scouring the platforms
— nid-nod heads, syncopating feet —
getting in before the day shift
of long brooms and sparrow clans.

And in the Railbar, human litter:
a roundfaced man moving soundless lips,
smirking at what they whisper;
a rocker cackling 'Me Mum's got cancer.
She's got massive tits. Cancer of the tits';
a thickset woman in a clean blue jumper
— greyhaired, with big teeth —
holding a stranger's lapels, tenderly...

Saying 'Talk to us; I need you.
Take us to Carlisle and bat me lug.
Why Carlisle? There's fields there.
I won't take your clothes off
till we're on the train, in the morning'.

Dawn comes up: the Baptist's head
on a dish huge with blood

Carlisle in flames

from the train, in the morning

MILL-HANDS: COLDEN VALLEY

Their houses were rubbished long since.
But the odd stack survives;
its tiered elegance competing with the poplars.

Stoop, step inside. It's like looking
up the barrel of a gun.
Stop, stroke a stone —
the soot of lives comes off on your fingertip.

What were they looking for, aiming at,
those old mill-hands —
trapped between stack and tomb
as the years loomed, the claustrophobia?

A loophole, touch of sky
like the one at the stack's top —
rare as a Saturday shilling?

And did they get it, ever?

Some time-slipped dinner break maybe,
when the press of sun gentled open the balsam,
its pearl-black seeds spattered their fissured palms,
and down gold air, looped on wisps of gossamer,
oak roller caterpillars did their Indian rope trick . . .

while by the fizzy blue beck edge
in impromptu crèches of moss and grass
(minded by the ones just too young for work)
kids crowed and gurgled,
spread fat fingers to the light.

But mostly it was otherwise of course:
mist-riders usurping the fells,
wind fallen like a tribe of Sioux
with yelping tomahawks to scalp the crags;

nights cold as Hebden cobbles
when, work-frozen, they must still endure
the supercilious monocle
of an overseeing moon . . .

and the beck, the beck always,
bumping, ricocheting down shelving rock,
running through their dreams as it did their days —

the beck that fed, clothed, drove them,
that boomed, slumped, fickle as trade
— in the end went on regardless
past their threadbare ghosts.

AUTUMN SALIENT

Black winds drive out among the hills.
Another leaf's shot down across the sky.
The sodden hedge has given up its frills.

In the stagnant fountain with astounded gills
the sun suppurates: a blinded spy.
Black winds drive out among the hills.

There was fruit, friendship, summer skills;
they're lopped, dropped, bitter-shy.
The sodden hedge has given up its frills.

Mist menaces the valley, kills
with a slow pillow consequence and cry.
Black winds drive out among the hills.

Mist is mouthing at eternal sills,
heaven's heraldry smoked out, awry.
The sodden hedge has given up its frills.

Look at the reed bed, its poisoned quills;
the season's on the block, the axe high.
Black winds drive out among the hills.
The sodden hedge has given up its frills.

KIN

My Uncle Bill with the silver plate in his skull
who taught me drill and how to knock off
imaginary Boche with a stammering Vickers
died daft as rabies trying to sup the Severn —
ten years after the war ended.

He was a moody charmer, hair thick as treacle,
with the absent swagger of a Cavalier
and a sporadic cough;
who as the whim pricked would make
the locals — only to spit them out
like spent cartridge cases.

To pay off family debts
— 'Our Flo, lend us a shillin' ' —
he'd sometimes take me out afternoons.
It always finished up in the club,
me in the shade with a soft drink,
him at the one thing that gave him cover —
his passion: snooker.

That way he could re-create, turf
the mud in his mind over with green,
swop shell holes and their human pulp
for netted pockets, coloured balls
that could be crisply fired yet never hurt.
The worst that could happen was a miscue —
so absorbed you forgot to chalk.

But when the floods, the mud returned,
he died with his medals, his silver plate,
out there again, as if he'd never been back.

SO THIS IS WHERE YOU ARE

Tabloids by the flower vase —
boobs, balderdash, flown in from Mars.

Your friendly hakim the houseman
flashing his syringe (School Of D'Artagnan).

Or Mary Magdalene to spike one's doss:
'Cuppertea?' at the foot of the Cross.

'To GH — last of the Bards'.
Those flowers from Seamus? Or De Sade's?

Hospital radio. Anything finer
in the Costa Del Angina?

Sisters Of Mercy. Agnostic scabs.
Feeders. Respirators. Bum jabs.

Destiny in a dog collar.
Greetings from the Ayatollah.

A monitor peaks and dips.
E.P. Catch him before he flips.

Sister's eye. Consultant's purr.
Scent of visitors. Chanel. Cri de Coeur.

Smell of pyjamas, sweat-sour.
An empty bed. Perfect, for an hour.

Stethoscopes attached to sahibs.
Death certs — up for grabs.

Another stiff? It's amazing.
No extra charge for double glazing.

That sideroom cowboy's raising Cain.
Old Ma Morphia due again?

Indwelling catheters. Dirty swabs.
Glasses for teeth. Mugs for gobs.

Diabetics slung with drips.
Paraplegics numb from the hips.

Last man to the bog's a wolly.
Fancy a trip on the drugs trolley?

A punk with an earring, cracked lips.
Gaffers who can't do zips.

Bits of heart, no longer fed.
Bits of time — as brusquely dead.

Jesus, let this clot disperse
in time to miss Thy next hearse.

ARTHRITIC

He'd sleep, but weight's pain;
the bones go on crying.
He'd love, but black frost's
in every cracking pore;
move, but each hauled inch
is another granite milestone.

He'd tracksuit out
of that bitter chrysalis,
dance o'er my Lady Lea
flash as a ghost, a raving butterfly —
but where's the god to strike the scaffold,
the skeleton key whose magic fits?

He'd swop it all, the chronic days
soused with cortisone or steel-pinned;
but who's to trade in plastic hips
or getting out of cars like a twisted spider?
Who can profitably stay
in a straight fight with an iron caliper?

Spontaneous death's a hope, not likely;
suicide a clenching shame;
and heaven could be anyway faithless,
a stratospheric Belsen, ruthless.

SHANGRI LA

Tea tray propped on her gasometer belly
the mad woman sits and burps;
shouts through her cheek at the blizzard telly,
babytalks to her saucer if it slurps.

Her confidante and medical adviser
is a small black cat;
her anathemas psychiatric nurses —
should one ever get past the mat.

When the voices tell her to, she sings.
Should they ask her to dance, she'll take the floor.
If they want her to play, that's it too —
hopscotch, in drippy drawers.

She could use any two of her nails for tongs.
Her hair's a mess of driftwood twigs.
When she bothers to wash, it's a flannel-push;
when she bothers to eat, green cheese or figs.

She is so happy.

STILLBORN DIALOGUE

Sperm said to egg
'I'm yours to beg'

Egg said to womb
'Could use the room'

Then heart to blood
'Dilate my bud'

And blood to heart
'Away man. Start'

Eye said to mouth
'Get out. Go south'

Nose said to ear
'There's only here'

Then nail to nail
'What's this then? Gaol?'

Gut said to crutch
'You up to much?'

Crutch said to gut
'I'd help you. But —'

Then knee whispered to knee
'Please, pray with me'

And thumb to thumb
'At least, we're dumb'

Skull said to skin
'Think we'll win?'

Skin said to skull
'You're beautiful'

Mouth said to feet
'So, what's to eat?'

And feet to mouth
'This caul. Your sheet'.

THERAPEUTIC ABORTION

'Father forgive us; we know what we must do'.
So in the starched light,
the ghoulish gleaming theatre,
with pity in the scalpel's lust,
with sickened bare obedience,
the sweaty surgeon, frozen girl
go through with their outrageous pact,
their mortal merciful offence.

Keep to kill or kill to keep:
the mad alternative that sprang
with cancer in a velvet breast
and now bears down upon the womb;
claiming as its angry due
life for life, a gristly inch:
sop enough to stay the mouth
of chaos, the precocious tomb

Nothing for the queasy pen
to wriggle out of or write off;
nothing for the tactful mourner's
muted, self-approving cough;
nothing but the nasty cut
of criminal necessity;
the barbarous, oblivious crux,
the absolute and bloody fact.

Nothing. The enormous act
of union and implanted love,
the self-surrender, fertile flesh
of passion and expansive trust,
trundled on a sudden trolley —
excavated, bundled back;
stitches over nothing, living
substance of a shroud.

Tomorrow squirming on a slide,
screaming up a lens' void;
swinging in a porter's bucket
gagged with dressings, dirty prayer;
tomorrow burning, blasted in
a furnace's abysmal breath;
tomorrow nothing, nothing but
exhausted ashes, shrivelled air.

Tomorrow crying down the sky,
crying for a son that was,
a guiltless guillotined that died
unripened, in his mother's blood . . .
risen like a cherub, calling
dove-soft from the hand of God:
'Forgive yourselves, my children.
As it was, I understood'.

FLESH AS GRASS

I watched them from the sheepwall at the hilltop —
the distant locals, leading hay.
There, in the dip, they'll graft no doubt —
badgering the stubborn bone
grunt, grimace, crack tattered jokes
— wondering the dusty while
if rain's to rip that edgy wrack
of thunderheads tomorrow or tonight.
There, it's work and nothing but:
iron-rations for the beast's remorseless mumbling;
winter-moody, in his dank, dung-splattered stall.
But to me, leant like this
on coping stones compact with history,
these gestures make a gallery of pride —
timeless, irrefutable.

The farmer scatters pronged lightning
with the prowess of St. George;
dragon-swathes green-foundering at his feet.
Some paces off the eldest son
strides out beneath a dripping truss
like a Ghanese chieftain with a high umbrella's
privilege of shade;
while further, on the piled cart
— an archetypal Ceres caught
superbly breasted, in the pageant of her prime,
the daughter: and over gold shafts
— iron-shouldered, oiled with sweat —
the great foam-fetlocked stallion, waiting
earnestly, against the cracking shout, the move . . .

Departing, the heart learns
such eloquence of their inspired necessity,
such rapt, explicit scripture of their ways,
it burns again with understanding of the sacrifice:
the dark firstborn raising ripe summer's body
— essential victim of his self-denying ecstasy —
for sun-investiture, strong fatherhood of light.
Decisively, the fall that seemed
annihilated grace,
is meaning-slashed, swift-power-thrust,
consistent, inexhaustible.
Coursing from the vast, the vivid

hunger of eternity,
it passes to impenetrate
all tissue of created things:
gleaming from the pheasant's eye,
streaming with the falcon's blood,
dark-flaming where the bull deploys
the thunder of its hardihood . . .
grass of being, realised,
voided, deep-transmuted then
illimitably sprung once more . . .
bearing in its plumy stir
seeds of substance, bones of breath . . .
resurrection. . . never death.

JEUX D'ENFANTS

The knack was fag cards flanged between two fingers,
wrist-skimming galleries where adults never came;
knockdown, scoop, the pasteboard dead
shuffled on to shoot again.

The knack was paper gliders: rooms of angles,
frail lightnings that lunged and swooped,
banged into panes like bluebottles, dropped
conker-abrupt.

The knack was paper boats careering like butterflies,
dodging down rapids, bucking weirs;
levelling off serene as swansdown, to lose
the eye in long horizons of rapture.

The knack was playing: airy
something and nothings, obliquely god.

VIRTUOSO

Walking the bathside, nothing fits —
those splayed haunches, that freckle-peppery skin,
the ellipsoid eyes, mongolian almost,
the bubble gum that blisters, fades,
the tinny transistor waffling on . . .

She sits, looks vacantly at the shallow end:
the squatting coach, his graceless minnows
doggedly thrashing their half-width;
then cuts the reggae, stows her cud,
in three bounds swift as a chamois
has bucked the startled board, is falling
sure as a snowflake to green beneath.

We see her supple, stalwart ghost
torpedo-sleek five feet below
then spiring to resolve itself
in a classic eight-beat crawl
— those crescent arms, slow, hypnotic,
that sotto voce drumroll of the feet,
never a bubble slurring the edge of her intent . . .

see her, how many times, shearing
with the stripped assurance of a dolphin
into acceptance, its melting instant;
the light tossing coins of acclamation
at the furrowed comets of her wake.

BOWLS

It could be my grandfather looking over that wall:
in the pouch of a grainy hand
flaking twist, nudging it round, down,
then pipe in teeth returning the scented rectangular tin
to the pocket of his Sunday suit before he struck his match,
fenced the sudden bud of flame, saw its glow dilate the bowl.
It could be my grandfathers yes, that solid dandy
known with defeated irony as 'Gentleman John',
looking quietly over the wall and smoking . . .
while the bell dripped like a bronze tap
 calling stragglers to church, and on the lawn
 cronies, feet on planted mats, slipped

the foxy jack to settle miles away . . .
and the sun lazed in fluted glasses down beside the seats,
and the woods ambled like stopping trains, Edwardian, endless...
every now and then clicking to glossy triumph
with a sound like the swill of milk in churns
or the wheeltappers of his working world —
before he sorted the goods from Shrewsbury to Crewe,
set the Acme Thunderer with its cork throbber
crisply to his stern mouth, heard
the massive first snort of the 8.15 moving off

FIXTURES

It can be hailing cabbages, raining rocks,
if there's a caseball among it there they'll be:
the touchline gaffers, the sawdust sourdoughs,
sticking it out to eternity.

And you'll hear them: clamped into Army greatcoats,
flatcapped, mufflered, assisting the ref:
'Mark 'im, Ted!'; 'Shoot, man, SHOOT!';
'Fetch 'im 'is Mam!'; 'Dirty — send 'im off!'

'Our Jack's lad' curling one in from a corner
makes their insteps quicken, their old toes tingle.
Plotting moves with beer-wet fingers on the table
— between dominoes — how they laugh, wrangle.

Chances muffed, openings taken,
every week an inquest (burial or resurrection);
and time the impatient space between matches,
the rage and relish of anticipation.

Nippers, they were never without a ball;
Rec or back street their dribbling nursery.
Dusk never fell but on a scrimmage
of midget jerseys in solemn fury.

And they're still at it: wheelchaired, on crutches,
trundling, stumping to their muscled praise:
the taste of glory, that ageless champagne,
in their bawling mouths, their seasoned, canny eyes.

SOMETHING ELSE

Where did he come from? Holton St. Mary? Cheam?
What was his culture? Wayout? Mainstream?
He'd flight the leg break like an architect's dream;
you'd no more resist it than a cat cream.

Had he substantial holdings? Or not a hope?
How was he with household chores? Could he cope?
You'd hear it spinning sweet as a gyroscope —
in the air somewhere, you could only grope.

Was he a womaniser, a wretch, a rake?
Did he do anything for heaven's sake?
It would drift down shy as a snowflake . . .
then off the pitch like a striking snake.

What was his manner? Airy? Curt?
Was he committed? Politically alert?
He'd gauge the damage like a demo expert;
you'd be down the blockhole before you'd tucked in your shirt.

Was he macho? Could he use himself in a brawl?
Or a gent, content to be just morally tall?
Slip and keeper's hands were snap-happy every ball
The castle was there; the castle would fall.

Was he never the least bit outré?
Did he rate even the teeniest hooray?
There was the flipper to nape at, the googly to play:
pads or short leg — a blob either way.

What was his temper like? Foul or fair?
Was he any kind of a father? Did he care?
He'd have your off peg slumped on air
like a seaside drunk in a deckchair.

Had he a gimmick, an edge, some private Zen?
What's he remembered for, more than other men?
He did a thing or two now and then.
Got the odd mention, something called Wisden.

EDEN

The apple tree was here before us;
at the leaf join a small bulge
— distinctive —
with each decided fruit.
Save for a few windfalls wasps dig
it's still like that;
compact, firm,
just a touch red.
But it's years
— the year she died, precisely —
since kids were at the thing;
we'd catch them spreadeagled
in snapping branches,
with appropriate outrage
send them catapulting off . . .
scared delighted bottoms bobbing,
some of the booty dropping as they ran.
Folk are kinder now.
No one steals the old man's apples;
even unbruised, with small bulges.

THE SIGN

It may come complete and scatheless
as a fruit, found one morning
on a bough suddenly blessed with being.

It may surprise in the tendril hand
of a child asleep: first word
of a new language.

It may be stumbled on:
a stone on a beach till then veined
with invisible runes.

It may be grey-haired —
yet come to birth
with a blue eye abrupt as heaven.

It can be posted on air, delivered
in a small hour, a great day:
the dream-child that is no dream;

that can never be and yet is
— beyond convention, bias, taboo —
the thing never to be told, that is;

that is a lack unfelt till present —
token of darkness, a brazen secret
writing itself by its own light.

It may be recognised
by the invalid it cures
with a kiss cool as a beech leaf

And no whisper, no backwards incantation
can swerve it ever
from its crucial instant —

arriving charged with sensuous adoration,
the radiant destiny of tribute,
to gain, grace, pass on.

PAYING BACK

Stones along a wall top;
chunky, irregular.
Some previous owner
must have set them up.
But what was their need?
Protection for his apple tree —
a sort of broken glass, operating
rather by indication than laceration,
against boys in the loaded rigging?
Something for shifty weather gods
to doodle on —
trim with a lichen fancy,
a bleached mosaic?
Or because the finished wall itself
looked so flatly functional?

I like to think, the last of these;
that without knowing substantially why
his making hands chose for him —
and rightly: fetching from the earth
till feel was profile, this frieze
bluntly individual.
I like to think he gave the sky
what it left him.

POEMS FOR HOPE

1

You slipped the customs.
No one knew you were there
till, tiny hijacker,
you took over: tucked, absorbed
in the fluent plane of her body
till the time came for declaration,
a compelled bearing, new land.

Words were foreign, message clear.
But you know me, you said.
How else am I here?
You heard me when your dreams coupled
— on the wind, above cloud —
the high white cry of the sandpiper.

Set me down, you said.
Bring me into my own
— any, every one's true country.
Let me cry, open my eyes
on free air, the doe grazing
sun-wide acres, the streams tumbling
from nippled rock.

Hold me, aeons-long.
Learn me, my gentle name.

In the bundling wind, thrushes sang.

2

The day you were expected, jets took the roof off —
a snarling wedge, scalding the sky with contempt.
And there you were: committed, tender —
the changeling, the thunder-calmer;
in your delicate, about-to-be hand
that unmatchable explosive: peace.

3

Before the flood, the obstinate dove,
that name invoked when you were womb-deep
— an older, abstract annunciation.

And now, to our rickety ark,
conferred by the flying beak of time,
this sprig, wand of new landfall, faith.

INCONSUMABLE

There can be no tomb for dead salamanders
such as love the flame.
When the last ember turns up its eye
those reptile ghosts assume an air,
a wind whose vehemence whirls up
another fire, another time.

No end rhyme for dead virgins
such as keep the flame.
Let once the leap of pride falter,
insisting with their astral thighs
they'll mend its brilliance, oil
to sudden sacred fire again.

No lying time for dead heroes
such as haunt the flame.
When the dragon beak drifts out, burning,
its last breath makes fire of water
till neither is: only sunset, huge,
dreaming its dying partner, dawn.

PSYCHOKINESIS

Take pylons, that swaggered yesterday
ambiguously awesome: beasts on stilts
like Martians dropped relentless overnight
or robots climbing with contemptuous efficiency,
science fiction stalking vividly to thrill —

these, now tolerated casually,
no longer snapped about by jealous curs
of rabid progress or too long leashed up aesthetics
but one with landscape, a prescriptive perch
for starling synods or the calm rook,

tomorrow may be obsolete as fossils:
skeletons of a prehistoric bird
whose triple tier of wings long since quite atrophied;
laid curiously, monumentally away
within some amber afterthought of passing sun . . .

theirs the fate of implements supplanted
by a new force whose flair's immediate:
a power of mind that has itself bright flesh,
a vast telepathy with meteoric fingertips,
bypassing as obtuse tautology

switch, plug, connecting wire;
scorning the bulb's transparent dignity;
its wands and wonders of precision drill;
as the wish burns, even, flashpointing
worlds of darkness to undying light.

OPTIONS

Shall I settle for a cat's pittance:
to be stroked, combed, cuffed, allowed
bonus bacon rinds, tail-tweaking kids?
Adopt open drawers, nap on old pullovers?
Chatty at glassy birds, be generally
here and nowhere?

Or shall I up and live with dolphins, travel
by supersonic ear, if the day's
horizon doesn't dress my whim
biff its beachball sun with a dismissive tail —
falling then through fathomless hatches ogle
my plumpness in weed-tentacled portholes?

Or is there somewhere, between beck and Bermuda triangle,
miaouling under the sleety stars,
a cat dolphin that looks like me —
a pedlar in flying fish, grey-whiskered, skittish,
sporting a sleek line, smelling nicer Sundays?

ONLY TOO TRUE STORY

The poet decided to get back to nature.
He rented a bedsit conservatory
and started to grow them, poems.
Early, they seemed such winsome elves;
he stroked, sang them swansdown lullabies,
measured their height daily, each towering, cherished inch.
Till one improbable day the thing kick-started;
brash as a mutant mafia they moved in.
One yanked him out of bed by the hair, shoved
a pen between his sleep-fuzzed fingers.
One tickled his ear, shouted 'Mine's a Terza Rima!'
A desert type, who hadn't liked a line he shot her,
bristled, needled him to change it.
There was one beneath his chair, drilling presumably for his anus;
another in the nick of his penis (wrong colour, of course);
a third under the bed, hissing Stalinist slogans.
He ran for the door. A crypto-creeper tripped him.
Made for the basement. A wiggly stem got up his nose.
Threw down his pen. Three telepathic tendrils
grabbed it, went into reproving sonnets.
One with leaves of money, spoony, glossy,
stroked his palm, told him not to worry.
One on stilts, who looked like a climber, brought him
coffee black as a sexton's fingernail.
One blared from the wall, a goldleaf ikon: 'Worship — or else!'
He rushed out, naked. A bonsai with a blanket
followed, put him on a circular bus.
He retired. Two of their voluntary visitors
asked after him, phoned for a publisher.
He wanted to die, they told him
not till you've written the really definitive one of us
about DEATH.

He was weak though, he died, went somewhere or nowhere.
Wherever it was, they cared; they waited for him.

THE STRANGEST THING

Cuts down trees
to say it shouldn't

smears oceans
to wipe its butt

builds a greenhouse
with aerosols

goes to the stars
to see if it can

loses its hair
over a sly growth

shoots up its kind
for a power fix

will scale an alp
to fetch a dog

allows God
to kill its enemies

worships gold
and baby's toes

lives on
a spinning surd

an expiring passport

animal

the strangest thing

GETTING IT STRAIGHT

Count your crosses, petal.
The wound is mortal.
And luck brittle.

Art's a cake for cattle.
Verse a vintage cripple.
Words not worth the waffle.

Faith's a parson's brothel.
Charity a broken bottle.
Hope won't fill a nipple.

Save your kisses, petal.
The hurt is foetal;
all else prattle.

Desire's a call girl's tipple.
Purity a tinker's kettle.
The sting's not half the nettle.

Truth's a bent metal.
Pity won't jam a rifle
or the next battle.

Cut your losses, petal.
The world is brutal.
And you little.

SEVERN MINNOWS

In the sun's strobe their quick silver
looks random as spilt nails —
yet each moves with acute control;
never touching, however curt
the space between.

They were the totems, devout joys
of my Shropshire childhood:
inches of glory risen
from pouncy nets and half sunk jars
to glittered sills.

'They won't keep, you know' said grownups.
I used to try, four days —
but could never win, before time
unforgivably some white gut
would surface, stop.

They were here when the troop trains went:
shoals flashing bayonets —
when the spare, khaki ghosts slopped back,
in and out of their smashed, wet skulls
like loose shrapnel.

They are here now, in the Bren's brisk
tock from Copthorne Barracks
— sound of a butcher chopping meat —
with no swans, only a river
lead-ripped, sad.

REFUGEES: BELGIUM 1940

That month the weather launched into brilliance,
a sun-blitz, ridiculous.
Our Field Ambulance was stood by
when they started to leak down the road,
a bizarre May Day Procession:
kids on scooters, tethered goats,
carts so jerrybuilt with chattels they lurched.
I remember girls in furs gnawing lumps of spud
and a woman with a white handkerchief
whose eye was red jelly.
Two cloaked poilus sat a Renault roof.
And nuns passed (maybe paratroops disguised).

Stukas had been their closest neighbours:
a machine-gunning yowling sound-track
sealing off the impossible past.
Now all they could do was move;
anywhere, so it was further off.
But quite a few spoke, some good English,
some pidgin — like the whores we'd known in Lille.
And more than one wished us luck.

Later, in an empty house,
we found a blackbird, caged.
Left as a talisman perhaps, to say
this wasn't really happening?
Or, with the backhanded cruelty of the victimized,
lust left?

And we, did we let it go,
to fly with shrapnel, sing for worms?

Dead questions. Soon buried.
Like Belgium, France.

BORDER BALLAD

Touching our soles with each other's
— that was erotic:
a spell of naked flesh, a holy game
that was its own inseparable province . . .
until the day the rocket fell.

I seem paralysed from the neck down.
If I could move, I could still touch
your sole, I believe — with this toenail
I feel is broken.

Are you stiff, like me?
Clothed like me in blood?
I want to reach you.
All that comes out is 'Mama'.
And, from across the floor, 'Water. Water.'

Mama Water, from whom we came —
who cannot even wash us away.

HISTORY LESSON

And there were giants in the earth in those days, children:
Strontium Pilate and Divine Caesium,
who never crucified a single subject
(bones were ash before flesh touched wood);
Asbestos the Elder, who conquered fire
simply by standing on people's chests;
and later, in the Christian spasm,
Krypton the Innocent, Cadmium the Good
— he invented, remember, the foetal minotaur . . .

So much for giants. Before you leave the room
zip up your lips, put in your walking lenses,
with your good hand screw on the fingers of the other,
check if your legpiece is in your satchel then
get on with your half lives.

CATATONIC

The clubfoot warden
stumps upstairs.

I sit, listen
to my stupor:

the dead clock
that won't stop.

This room, this ruin,
is it mine —

or the rancid
opposite?

Shake hands, it says
— offering two

frayed naked
fingers of wire.

Have you a soul?
it says.

Cut your wrist,
find out.

Rain's at the window,
a swarm of snakes.

Gas hisses.
Conspiracy, voices.

Is it me,
these gnarled roses —

this smiling
severed head?

THE GLASS PEOPLE

Sometimes you see them flitting in procession
— cool, intent, upright —
like thermometers moved by invisible hands,
that do not reflect common speech, only
each other's mercurial, naked thought.

Sometimes they swarm: to hang tinkle —
a chandelier of deft falsettos.

Sometimes they're just backs of heads
sly as periscopes cutting the water.

With always, gesticulating somewhere around,
their chapped, tongueless helots.

Are they annealed or born?
Where, among the ice and corridors,
do they mate, if they ever do?

These are glassy questions.

IT

It was like another mouth, salivating.
It was a thing of hair, a soft cannibal.
It went into strange beds for comfort
and ate to a noise of sobbing.

It was like another mouth, that lived to bleed.
It turned explosive wands into dribbling worms,
would scrap a moon
for a smiling whim.

It was like another mouth, that bled to live.
Repetition was its immortality
What it vomited in time walked
and had its own mouth.

ARMADA

the mallards waddle
into the garden from the beck
stooping and beaking everywhere

is it a dream he has
she was in the room   certainly
that absence is her scarf that used
to coil like a snake
round the chair back

one of the drakes begins to hustle
she seems to be running away
but is she going faster to take him with her
and there's another drake
barging in from the side

when will she return if ever
he strokes his chin should have
shaved today in case she came back
there is a shadow in the mirror

the mirror of the beck
into which a duck plunges
but cannot miss the hard fury
pegging her trying
to put one over on her

did these drakes appear
when she was with him
or are they a strange dado
not like things on a nursery wall
but merciless people
think they're lovely
don't look down their mouths

he is on her she
is soused beneath him
you'd think she'd drown
how do you drown in a mirror

that was it

that's it.

PARTING

is a brute
with a tucked, mean eye
and a sheaf of I.O.U.s;

haunting playgrounds
for a tossed ponytail,
a snatch of early laughter;

weeping rust and cinders,
tearing up iron photos,
eating its ring.

DIVORCE

The children are hanging mobiles.
Yesterday it was crayoned fish;
today, mummy and daddy:
black twine through the paper skulls
and no eyes.

Did they forget to put in the eyes?
Some time ago the phone rang –
a woman's voice.
It will ring again, a man's.

Or did they put them out?

SWEETS OF EROS

Slugs.

A skin of caramel
proceeding
with the suave elegance
of a liner
leaving an estuary

or the tiny strap
of liquorice
seen on paths
at dusk . . .

There,
confection ends.
One thinks
of tongue-rasp —

and the sunflower
leant out of the sky,
a mast
wrecked on a reef.

Eggs
in damp turnups.

That slimy blur.

GENITALS

A matted slit, a turkey's nose —
sometimes they don't seem a part of one;
of the human race, that is.

Other times, they are the race —
ache and strut,
there's just nothing else.

One day perhaps they'll atrophy:
it'll be sperm-banks
and womb-safe deposits.

Only, it won't be funny any more —
me with no fandangle,
her unpunctured.

What we'll do for orgasms
I daren't guess.

Maybe our washing machines
will have them for us.

STEPDAUGHTER

She talks with flip omniscience
about 'having it off':
something adults do —
bizarre, boring.

At times however condescends
to brief us. Grateful, we find
'bugger' means screwing dead people,
'castrate' to cut off one's willy.

She's thirteen. Needs a bit
of casual reassurance.
Like it won't affect her
she's got us, remember.

Like that's just video nasty stuff,
worked up to provoke a thrill.
'Ugh!' She shudders with crisp relish,
goes off into fantastic defences . . .

only nut cases, bare-bummed hairies
in rain forests . . . and even there
always the rainbow,
the flung rope, Tarzan.

Later she'll learn
— pray Christ, impersonally —
it can all happen —
nearer home.

WITH STUDENTS

Others are asking others questions,
or listening hands cupped round chins.
futures swimming in their immense eyes.

Me they don't want.

Should I be latching on then.
provoking or boring them into speech?

I give up. Drift around
comprehensively superfluous –
to beach at last in achieved limbo:
that cave of the arrived, stupendous image
the emigré photographer's studio.

A glossy inset tacked on pinboard
has come unstuck.
One of its pages lurches out,
dragging at the rest.

Outside, a grasshopper whets its scythe.

Someone with quiet hands has locked the door.

TEENAGER

When I had my heart-do
she went up to her bedroom
— so I'm told —
and cried, hours.

Now, three years on,
I don't know her:
all baths, aerosols,
going out —

a guerrilla in some bizarre unit
on her way to storm
— what do they call it —
maturity . . .

in her armoured, other life
about as forthcoming
as a tortoise
with lockjaw . . .

grabbing at shoes, cash,
borrowing, cadging
going out,
always going out

to march the streets,
squat cafes, bars,
with her tittery, hard
clone sisters

only if she's skint staying home,
then to some cat-yowling tune
above a bass thumping
like a sick headache;

in a tip of cuddly toys,
bighearted valentines, smeared cups,
and the robotic drone
of a hair drier.

It used to be horseplay,
spoof clinches,
pet names, a spatter
of blue jokes.

Now she's trampled on all that,
slung out diminutives,
is exacting status,
her proper title —

honour from those
whose apparent duty's
to oblige
her every whim:

automats who owe her,
must stand, deliver
everything from crisps
to lip gloss, pronto.

Eventually, I'm told,
they come back to you;
assuming
you still want them.

EXECUTORS

Cousins. The one with the tonsure,
the one with thin lips, big teeth,
the one with acne scars

hypertensive, of a line prone
to strokes and heart-dos

who've lasted, by chance and charity,
so far

and now — having shaken hands
over the riven past;
buried its quaint, stupid differences,
spells of misunderstanding, even hate —

unite in tacit rueful competition
to see who's next

each posed to bequeath to the others
what they once shared intact

each holding trembly-fingered
deeds of that dapper haunt of childhood
the doll's house

the magical condemned property
burning invisibly
a room at a time

soon to fade

from the frozen site

GET THE EARLY WORM

Snuff it quick
death's a diploma:
a pukka passing out parade —
bouquets by the barrowful
soigné groans
everyone there you ever knew
from Shakespeare to the Dalai Lama.

Snuff it slow
death's a two-timer:
skinny as a Grunewald nude —
no meat for the sorrowful
a tune on the bones
everyone there you never knew
saving TTFN to a chunk of coma.

TERM TIME

Images we showed excitedly at break —
jarred trophies: a sapphire beetle,
a butterfly that flapped epileptic eyelids,
a twist of grass snake — green vein
in a marble — a minnow darting silver, veering.

Images that time saw differently —
museum pieces: a cyanosed smear,
a thorax pinned on scrounged cardboard,
a limp, niffy snatch of rope
— and like a new moon floating outrageous,
a stiff, salt belly.

SLIPWAY

by the grave
the frieze of grief

posies
black gowns

a child turned
into someone's heart

a lopped father

filing to the brink
dropping their jots of earth

a man's eyelids fluttering

the blue stare of the woman beside him
glinting wet

and after that kingfisher moment

the sheer atlantic of fells

the chosen

under secret orders

in his one man submarine

waiting to lose flesh ballast

swim with the skull

MONGOOSE ON HIS SHOULDER

GODSON

Child of spasmodic arms
and smeared woollies
tumbledown walks
and few, loved words

the world's whim
leave you tonight
kind as your puckered thumb
its pillowed mouth.

Slip from day's bough,
your mother's kiss,
like a wind-touched
seed of ash —

to lie straight as a sunbeam,
clean as snow,
in sleep's downy
calendar.

Angry voice
and jealous toy
vanish
from your bedside;

mutant spider,
wolfish ghost,
powerless in moonlight
fade.

May breezes pour you
dreams soft
as sugar
from endless canisters;

let the house
glow quietly about you
(snug as a turtle's egg
in its warm sand);

and tomorrow wake
like new bread;
crust for a top tooth,
buttered and lavish, good.

THE BALLOON

When I was six (and naughty)
God came to call;
stood at the lane end, in the air;
not moving, simply there.

Radish-red, angry,
taller than I'd ever thought;
taller than our cherry tree —
and broad, against that cobalt sky.

He looked as if he'd never move;
still, like me. But he did
— slow as a jellyfish —
down, down towards me

then up, straight over,
showing his black mouth, beneath;
pulling my eyes out wide with him,
bigger the smaller he went.

'Humph. Humph' was what he said
— gargling, snorting fire —
'Humph. Humph' over the tiny houses,
the quiet hill.

A SEAT IN ARCADY

Our back lav was a smooth wooden hole
in a whitewashed shed

and was the family island. Summer days
you'd go there with 'The Wizard'
and forget time.

In the corners would be hieroglyphs
of dead spiders

the scent of wallflowers
would come in from the garden

and the seat be warm.

In the glass porch that served as a greenhouse
they'd be shelling peas;
shooting them into cool white bowls.

And when you pulled the chain
it would wait — like someone with a stammer —
then gush:

a soda water syphon

only deeper

stronger

slower

NEW BRIGHTON FERRY

You were eight years old, on the New Brighton boat.
You had watched the quayside sailors, blind to their own miracle,
unpinning eight coil hawsers from bollards, to hurl them
idly as snake charmers to the teak palms
of the sailors on board. . . who in hangy jerseys and gulping boots
stowed them, went striding off.
You were astern now, waiting for screws suddenly to thrash, lather.
Then turning with the ship, the dinosaur cranes grazing the docks skyline.
The gold bell shone from the bridge. You could see the Captain.
Below, like piano hammers, engine rods glistened, fell.
The ship was faster than its bows, fast
as the sparks tearing back from the funnel.
You went gunwale to gunwale, wild as a squirrel,
you couldn't miss anything — from the bucketed dredger
to the tramps, tankers, coming hugely in.
You were five, spelling out letters on sterns,
seeing who'd shout the answer first;
seven, picking out ocean flags
to check with your fag-card album at home:
a changeling, on fabulous water, one
with the globe-strutting lion, the white star.
Any moment now the ship would be a tug
with a liner slid solemnly at heel,
the place Lisbon, Acapulco. Off New Brighton pier
the one legged diver was stumping his iron ladder,
climbing the sky, as he always would,
to fall deathless as a rainbow.
You were eight years old. Never, never coming back.

CUNARDERS

I'd hear them in the night, baying like stags
over the sleeping forest of small boys
that was Liverpool, down past the Crosby lightship
where the sea-drunk bellbuoys wagged their star-struck heads.

I'd draw them in my rough books, with coloured funnels,
make impossible models of them in chunky wood
that capsized in the bath but always came up streaming,
exultant as dogs with sticks in their teeth.

Mauretania, Berengaria, Aquitania — these were never
keel-blocked skeletons Meccano-pieced together,
straitjacketed with cunning rivets, plates —
but avalaunched epiphanies out of some triton's head.

Their soundscapes built my youth, were my long gods —
always in the offing, never wharf-trussed;
those twelve ton anchors, those burly sirens
commanding even the spouts and flukes of white whales.

They were everybody's, yet peculiarly mine —
mine and the Liver Bird's that green-tiptoed to see them,
their smoke, their hulls, the Mersey that breathed to hold them,
coming in from everywhere, across the world.

HOPES

My daughter slouches in from school,
chucks her satchel anywhere,
and belts upstairs to sluice in pop —
something she wants to do, at last.
An hour later, the stereophonic air
still cauliflower eared,
down she bounces, cheeps a kiss at me,
shouts 'Dirty old git' and cuffs my head
then is away to the piano and Mozart —
like someone trying to tightrope
in Wellington boots.
As abruptly, she stops in a mirror,
counts freckles, wishes
they'd constellate elsewhere,
and complains that her sister,

to whom she writes secrets,
and who's elder, towns away,
does not reply.
Bucking those brandysnap curls she states
— sforzando — she's sick of being laughed at, even
her tentative eye shadow melting into comedy.
Tangerine-breasted, half ripe
— so much the worse for cramped longings —
she wants a youth to prove her flesh,
a job to give her point, impact:
all she gets is a grunted litany . . .
what's the past tense of reçevoir
if x equals five and y is constant
compare Hitler Mussolini Stalin
hands up who knows . . .
Parking her legs on whoever's nearest
'Why don't you do something for me?' she cries.
Do something for her? In our protective dotage,
what? Time on time we've thrashed things through,
and this seems it: at most
set her off like a yacht seawards,
hoping she'll get there, however slant . . .
that no devious wind exploit and drop,
no bumptious brawling wake capsize;
if she cares — and she will —
hoping her life outride
its spumy challenges without buckling, rust;
that no clannish weed slack-off her style;
no sun stood over warp and sear;
that she's never escorted home
with an ogre's blessing branded on her prow . . .
shades of Hitler, Mussolini, Stalin . . .
but makes landfall in the wisdom of a latitude
still near enough for love.

INDIAN ROPE TRICK

Silence. Noon. The tower of sun, its rapt, circled crowd.
Central they stand: the stripped fakir in his tall, snailshell turban;
the chosen boy, in a twist of loincloth, the borrowed, sacred mongoose in his
        hands.
The man bows assent to sun, than splaying hands exact as a conductor's
stares tense as a burning glass at cracked, immediate earth.
And from that dusty foot of ground it comes,
from the risen evocative crescendo of his hands:
a rope white-taut as a king python, charismatic, determined.
The mongoose runs, the boy leaps, locks thighs over, clinches feet,
begins to swarm; proud, deliberate.
And it grows with him, that white snake, every stretched handhold surer,
        firmer,
till lost eyes tipped back below see pink, clinching soles go lighter,
fade, dissolve into that white stalk, that taut irreversible taper . . .
till there is no mast of shadow sloped from the watchers' forgotten feet,
only the trick that's never done:
the sky blue and plate-bare but for a vapour trail of sloughed skin;
in the distance like a sidling leaf what could be a slipped loincloth –
in the ring a crosslegged veteran at prayer,
and a turbaned youth walking off with a bright-eyed mongoose on his
        shoulder.

GEORDIE STARLINGS

I walked out of Central, (Yggdrasil to you,
best squat you ever had),
and there you were: Sturnus Vulgaris –
into the brickwork thick as currants on a cake;
cramming, crocketing arch and pilaster,
swagged on flagropes, a couple even
in the tuck of Poseidon's keystone beard.
I walked out to the right, your waste hit me –
stench and substance, some still wet,
a splashy tidemark round the lower ashlars.
And were you yammering! Turned on, I suppose,
by the sodium lighting – anyway squirting, seething –
a scrimmage of sun-boozed crickets
ecstatically out of tune, time.
Oh, I'd seen you at home, half a dozen or so
parading the lawn with that polka dotty walk –.
But this, this yobbo gatecrash,

Blackpool bucketed on blameless Newcastle —
how was it, how had it come about?
Had you arrived one fanatical day
like supporters for some World Aviary Cup
and dug the gig, drunk it so much you stayed?
What did you eat, and where? Was life
so much of a bird-brained holiday you didn't have to?
Like a Sunday painter's, a drippy pointilliste mess around?
And sleep, did you never sleep, or only in snacks?
I walked out and beyond the slabbed precincts
till I came to the clock of St. John The Baptist;
thinking I'd find you — stuck for a laugh —
on the slow see-saw of its minute hand.
But it was tilting towards avalanche alone.
A swish above, like rain swooping,
and there, on the churchyard trees, I saw you:
those gaunt survivors suddenly coniferous
with your massed, magnetic settling.
Jack-knifed into silence, there you stood:
a mute chorale, communion of saints
in plumed humility too close for contradiction;
transfiguring the catacombs of boughs
your heavenly droppings had bleached, purified.
Sturnus Vulgaris? More like Angelicus, that hour.

HERE AND HEREAFTER

Here and hereafter the table,
furrowed like a twice grown fingernail:
its glass-marks planetary orbits,
its knots a scatter of suns —
with me leant over it
like God above a sky map.

Lifting my head I see a recessed window,
frosted like a thousand umbrellas;
part of a cell, the plain deal allowed me
to practice my haunting art.

Here I sit, the wind's hurly burly,
sputter and frying of rain outside —
sit and work, remember my trapped forbears . . .
what of these, the monks, that had no windows —
whose self-inquisition forbade such fripperies;

who kept their place, their few yards of freedom,
disciplined as palace sentries;
touching-in their velluminous missals,
their allegorical higher case —
sometimes on knees arthritic with prayer
slanting the world to steepled fingertips —
or hailing Mary with beads of days
bright as rosehips on Her singing, virgin tree.

And I like to think that whatever nonsense
sophistry involved them in, faith absolved:
those moments when plaster flaking from the roof
to stain such a table as this
might have been something else: droppings
of that white fantail the Holy Ghost,
over their shoulders passing wise as salt
to freeze in flawless grace,
honour the grain at their aching, blessed elbows.

SOUTH PIER: BLACKPOOL

Kids are dolphins bouncing a swell of lilos,
the sheltered gaffers gnarled iguanas.
Pinballs dribble delirious slaloms,
bikers spit-bomb a spade and its castle.
Past tripping floats a tyre-fendered smack
putters out to sea.

In her booth tiled with flashlit skulls
here's Gipsy Fortune, wrinkled, ageless,
conning motorway maps of hands
— spaghetti junctions, fast lanes.
Silver-palmed mostly, dispensing hope —
with an occasional bandaged truth slipped in . . .

And while the turnstiles tick, the bingo barks,
there, last day away from home
and simmering factory fat,
it's the Barnsley lot: battered fish
who've had their chips for another, smashing year:
deckchair-sprawled, a claque of happy losers,
licking salty wounds, sharing a wisp of sun,
a final cornet, bit of familiar backchat.

TARN BIRDS

A clarinet falls out of a cloud.
Curlew. Straight as skiers,
in a foamy rush,
three swans touch down.
Moorhens are tiptoeing shallows.

Wagtails shuttlecock between stones.
Coots pip, parp about.
A pennywhistle sandpiper cries.
Swifts pick off the middle air.
Rough, brief, a drake locks on.

Carpet-beating the spluttered water
three swans taxi, take off.
Circle once, go over —
the tarn like an ear sipping
the lost whine of their wings.

BLACKBIRD

You look new every time. It's as though
we had you for Christmas, out of the sky's stocking:
mole-smooth coat, banana-bright bill,
gold-rimmed eye like a tiny curtain ring —
all for a spatter of crumbs on a window sill.

Well, it's January now, and here you are
jabbing your tongs at old biscuits,
while a snowflake or two, so unsure
they seem to drip rather than fall,
flouts the pale blue upper sky.

You choose the biggest scrap. Prising your beak apart
it teases your throat like a dare
then gulp, you've conquered, flown.
Not that you fence-sit —
ten minutes, you're back again, trusting, hungry;

not one to waste anything, even me.

THRUSH

Before dawn's even looked
through sleep-tucked lids
he's there

knocking me up

rattling notes in the palm of his voice
like a champion dice thrower

convincing me with his brilliant crap
that luck's belief,
there's a sky behind the sky
just asking to be sung.

They claim he does it
defending what he's got.

Who needs defence
that can broach a noise like this?

Shakespeare? Too many words, it says.

Triple sixes, that's what life's about.

Moments, not a stretch.

Me: what I shout.

HAIKU

Rain on the roof.
The silver birch
has fresh buds.

Has the wind fallen off
its tightrope?
Your clothes-line's so still.

Lost for an audience
I looked up —
to reproachful stars.

An owl's cry.
All at once
the snow's hill.

Snow. The phone ringing
in an abandoned house.
Time-warped grasshopper.

Against the thunder cloud's
echoing shadow
a butterfly.

Is that a petal
falling from the moon?
Earthquake, hold your breath.

Dusk. Half-naked flesh
of day dissolving into
night's Eurasian arms.

Rain tapdancing
on a left out table.
A bored frog.

Falling asleep
after lovemaking.
The last snowflake.

CHURCH BRIC-A-BRAC

I have decided I don't want

amputated effigies in tandem
cased bones of some interfering duke
fonts wooden with doves on pulleys
rollcalled heroes buried by range finder

but the woman in flat shoes
at the centre of the rood screen —
let the gold cross enter her

KITE MONDO

Cloud-face, I shout, old weirdie in the wind —
how do you keep that high?

You look as if you hadn't heard.
Then palpably, a pigtail shakes.

In view of oriental precedent
perhaps I'm hardly ceremonious?
Well then, another try:

O Longchinned Master Of Meticulous Enlightenment,
Moon Of Metaphysics, Gnomic Arbiter —

In vehement koan you butt sideways.

So I'm pompous, not sharp enough eh?
Have to be nudged to stay with you,
nudge back to meet your play?

Pigtails in pokes should be
chased out of it, I cry.

That pleases. Back you sway, righted, serene again.
Pressure, only by pressure, you say.

Walk towards is fadeaway;
walk back is slant the higher.
So you have me, on a tall string . . .

You or Me, you say.
Pressure, only by pressure, breathing
like a carp against the stream, you say.
Inhale the illuminated moment,
rise with it . . . isn't that the Way?

Cloud-face, old sky-teaser,
the children have tired of you. Not I.

MALE SEA HORSE

Camouflaged, sunk in
the colour of what you're hooked to;
doodling a filament, a sudden tuft
to match the wavy pattern of the weed
– when you detach to prowl your chosen furlong
you may look like nothing so much
as an eighteenth century vac
but it's apposite, the image –
and with those eyes, smart as searchlights,
round as geiger counters,
you don't miss anything;
not the slightest edible scrap.

And when you couple, she rounds on you,
shooting a million eggs into your pouch,
it's only a month and you're giving birth:
clones, a thousand-a-day marathon
jerking out to litter the sea spaces
pale as dandruff.
It would be like a boy blowing bubbles
if the effort weren't so patent.

Hippocampus. Half horse, half caterpillar.
It's come down to us, that hybrid monogram,
in a mint of hefty, stipple-engraved tomes.
But you are more than that:
a cabbalistic baroque key
to the only text, the book of what is.

So that, gazing on you, each of us feels
taken up by something that's for him alone:
a wonderful, unrepeatable toy,
talisman, quotation of deity –

and wants to die into you,
in thought about you.

IT WAS

It was to do with a pin-legged finch
on a sill, looking for bread.

It was to do with light slipped in at a window,
the soft bounce of sunbeams on a wall;

with a bareheaded stranger on a ferry
seen crossing to the other side.

You were to leave it on the kitchen table,
invisible, as it always was;

go back to sleep, into your wrong life,
until it summoned, wanted you once more —

stroking with fine-haired meanings
you didn't realise till time caught up.

It was to do with tenderness, washing over you
deft, delicate as wind;

with otherness: the summer ghost
of a hand cool on your shoulder

and angels: so ripe with light
you could walk through one without ruffling an atom.

To do with everything: the naive surd,
the holy riddle that

— still there whether you knew it or not —
somehow left you clean . . .

to do with blessing, how one should be, was.

VICTIMS

Last night — she does it quite often now —
death came again to my bed.
Long legs, Kashmiri eyes,
a mole on her left eyelid.

Strange. How she's half my age
yet has time for me, her current pet —
(in the dark hear that watch I bought her:
a lapping, jewelled cat).

She kisses, calls me a dewlapped old twerp,
kisses, tweaks the lobe of my ear;
kisses, says she misses me
— and will — when I'm no longer here.

Teases me about my bald patch
— monkish impotence, for sure;
draws me a spine's length with her diamond nail,
digs me deftly, wantonly, elsewhere.

Sometimes it's tickle and run, like a spider;
Sometimes a nip like a kitten's, wild;
then all at once cleaving tight with love:
a needy, frightened child.

I twit her about her white hairs,
one for each folded, camphored lover;
manfully boast I'll soon outlive her —
sudden, not a smile.

She makes me happy, watching her frisk and flicker
— a sea swallow between breakers' roar.
Makes me sad. For her, not me —
what by staying I'll do to her.

GONE

Did he know her before?
Was it just that night?
Ask the sky.
The road was white.

Did no one see her
along the lane -
coming cold, cold
as a winter moon?

Was there wind that night?
Not to shift a slate.
What was the road like?
The road was white.

Did they take the ford
by the old spire?
They took the ford. A dead
lamb lay there.

Was there a reason?
No reason.
She came to claim,
cold as a winter moon.

Is his wife there?
There, alone —
bald as frost,
stiff as a headstone.

And the children?
Grown. Gone.
Only thistles now,
the wild cat's den.

Who's asking?
The frozen cup.
Who's heard?
Wind, it won't stop.

WINDOW SEAT

Dawn. On the wall outside
wind-chimes whose slaty carillon
last night trickled,
caressed my ears
like a bijou by Ravel.

Twitching: a mole-gibbet.

And the roses whose nodding scent
disarmed me the same evening —
what do they hold now
but the family cat: a clawed wind
about to hit the wagtail
on the golfcourse lawn.

Metaphor, you strolling miracle,
any minute, any mortal second —

what a perfect mess of things!

VETERAN

They've bypassed the farm now.
But if you stray wisely, sure enough
you'll find the byre, rusty
hand-shears on the sill,
and the stalls where milk from stubby teats
hissed clean into tin pails,
and the suede-skinned Freisians shifted, backed —
that months before cargoed with child would slouch
down lanes starred with cow parsley,
their breath a malty fume
of clover-shouldered meadow grass —
where the old farmer, buttoned neat to the neck,
strode his tilted, sheepish acres;
martially whistling his flattened dog
to up, nip those sloppy heels.
I worked for him once, a long vacation,
tossed hay, trod it down in the barn

(it was ripe, lush as a woman's flesh)
with his lad, whose only thought
was racing bikes and getting drunk weekends.
We'd take bread and cheese, bottled tea, in the field;
he'd scold, the old man, keep us all at it,
but sometimes talk . . . about the menace, happen,
of green hay, whose sweaty smoulder might erupt, flare;
about Spare Time — something that lost you, made you think —
(he'd read a book , once, other than the Bible);
and openly about the folly of a lad
who hadn't yet acquired so much as boots.
Bad weather, he thought, came not for sin
but to test the stoic muscle.
What was manual, rhythmic, must be holy.
There was only one real devil: a stamping bull —
(against that he'd puff a vehement pipe).
So it went: meanwhile, work was life —
clipping spreadeagled tups, lopping the pirate thistle,
righting endless lengths of wall . . .
even on Sundays when the psalms he'd whistled
a hard week rose up in tenor strength
to tread the raftered diapason like joyful feet on hay.
'He's a good companion, God', he'd tell me.
And if you stray further, round a bit,
you'll find the water trough —
and the motto, moss-tagged but distinctive still:
'He that drinks from this spring shall go on
with his head erect'.

SEA HORSE

What has gentleness like yours to offer
the glazed impenitence of neighbours —
the lionmouth's fancy dress of daggers,
clenched smirk of the alligator?
Half sailor, half adagio gymnast,
accepting, clasping, connecting all,
your courteous ghost moves among the masts
of seaplants, the stone flowers of coral.
Like a clef's your tendril of a tail
anchors in music, a key of dream
where lovers drift like flute melodies;
so slow their tracery's almost a frieze . . .
their constellated profiles seem
unicorns of glass, so airy, frail.

YOU

For years you slept on top of the bookcase,
launching from the sofa-back
smack into it, that rosewood cornice
recessed unwittingly when my uncle carved the thing.
It was your party-piece; tight as a pole jump.
Sometimes, to amuse visitors, we'd edge you into it —
stampede a little, to watch you concentrate regardless
then thump success: black-pipped golden eyes
brimming the tiny, reverberant parapet.
You were a ham, admittedly; you loved it —
like me poking you with a probe of grass,
you'd growl, scream six yards suddenly off then lie
with fuming anticipation for the wand to dig again.
Not that you lacked precision; should I stroke too deep
you'd nip in with a lovebite judged to a centimetre —
and should you be really annoyed swan-hiss,
click your anger like billiard balls colliding.
(And you could be elegant; that plume of a tail
thrilling, even when only making water).
Here, scoffing fish and chips,

it seems strange not to save you any
— like taking communion alone —
those flakes of cod like wafers,
bits of the Redeemer you're no longer up to.
You could do worse though, than where you are,
between the spendthrift blossom of apple and cherry,
the blackbird's contralto drawl.
'Than where you are' — was that what I said?
When the grass parts to small, warm winds
I look for the one that's brindled.

OEDIPUS AT NEWMARKET

Wind splits the mare's tail
like palm-fronds under its belly.
Its mane challenges —
something out
of helmeted Thermopylae.

Four of its legs prod bonily off
then rush.
It's that tomfool of a foal again,
trying to straddle her
at right angles.

FROM THE CHINESE

I have been drunk for ninety years.
Tomorrow brings jade pills.
My ignorant son the baldheaded tailor
has stolen my flute for his lover.
The river flows into the sky.
There is plum blossom at the tip of my nose.
When my big toe uncurls
I will write another poem.

THE VILLAGE
(after 1930s Auden)

Precinct of inbred, marvellous options,
where the poacher mends the bobby's bike
and the Vicar is ridiculous on Mondays;
where the antediluvian cockroach
develops amazing properties
and enchanting bastards sprout like goosegrass;
before the inhabitants move to China or next door
take your pulse, cross four fingers.

Though you are happy today with the raffles
and oxygen of whist and coffee mornings,
though the fireproof caterers have arrived
to serve ortolans galore on the radiant lawn,
the sexton's big toe says rain,
the cross-eyed postman is checking his leads,
the Squire's lady has gone into black tights;
once again an outrageous demure woodlouse
prepares to detonate the safe.
And like history, its gigantic fable,
bowlegged, advancing on all fronts,
the burning fell stalks towards you.

WET DAY

Stapled to boredom, the poisonous fag
of a pen between smudged fingers,
I look out at the garden. Or, rather, don't look.

Because — who's kidding who?
Me, not rain's the trouble.
Rain's for looking into, not merely at.
For hearing, not just assenting to.

Hiss of dynamos, decisive, ceaseless.
Leaves that flicker like trout rising.
A tiff of wind, cross-hatching
above the spoked beadwork of a web.

That border whose dark soil
will open tomorrow like a piano lid
on a sound of flowers.

DIALOGUE IN THE SMALL HOURS

A.
Ragged gown looped over one arm,
begging contemptuous dark to hear my sins,
I talk a hole in night.
Chalk squeaks on the blackboard. I say,
to an Open University of echoes,
'Attention please; this is me:
your ultimate lesson in self-disgust.
Who tipped his wheelbarrowed brother out
on the hedgehog pebbledash?
Who refused his harelipped cousin
under the mistletoe?
Who went out to dances instead of nursing
his uncle's cancer — and danced on his grave?
Who ditched friends for money, burnt
healthy lovers from him like leeches?
Who stroked the wallflower ears,
smiled at the slavering hound?

B.
But you are accepted. Why undersell yourself?
This present familiar driving to his morning desk —
laundered, courteous, (yet brusque when juniors need it);
thoughtful about his secretary's birthday (and her knees)
would posthumously merit any kind of gold clock.
Tick off your virtues. You never jump in with the Union,
you can respectfully argue with the boss over a pint,
you have been known to give a successful party,
you are a good timekeeper. Not server; I didn't say that.
Relax. Take a pill. It's only three a.m.

A.
Who's this I'm talking to? Silver fish? Mice?
Should I spend my days then dealing only
with a shuffled pack of telly images?
Carting conboys of kids to mini-Disneylands?
Sniping at the neighbours' prinked cars and fish tanks?
Or taking a stealthy microscope to the dance of the DNA —
rinsing vision in the crystal of a dewdrop,
riding the rapt bourdon of the OM mantra,
talking through lotus navels, finding if he's HE . . .
projected fiction, protected surd?

B.
You have an apple tree. Bevys of crocuses
still honour spring, their buoyant regatta
of strutting periscopes and tossed coracles
taking its green effervescent wave never a month
later than sworn. Your fences may wince
at the thrashing gales but nothing splits their sockets.
June will burst from last year's stems
to take the air in a signal flush of roses.
You will look out on the gnarled boughs
of September offering its sane fruit,
and where the treehouse rope, the pendulum of childhood,
swings tirelessly over the compost marl
say yes, I have an apple tree.

THE LEAPING POOL

TRADE

The girl on the cheese counter offers me a taste.
"Irish or German?" I could give her forty years.
"No matter," I say, strenuously offhand.
"Have the cheapest, then?" She brings it out of glass.

Cornflower eyes deftly appointed with mascara;
skin a bit coarse but scrubbed to the vivid blood;
lipstick that doesn't ever crinkle over;
third finger left hand a ring of plain gold.

With easy precision she slices it down.
"Four ounces do?" then with a shake
flicks a bag open, in a skywriting hand
— not really perhaps — wraps, writes me off.

As to dress, she has the strength and tact
— only a tiny gold chain above her scalloped blouse —
to know what not to say . . .
a sense of space, Chinese almost.

To lie with her would be like eating a tulip.
Nor do I want to know her name, opinions.
What's best left out's the thing, makes
an image I might have chosen, right.

TAKEN

Whistling, she was fierce as a robin;
running, crisp as a wagtail.
She'd but to clear her throat, a dove spoke.

Her smile was a shot of sun through leaves;
her pout a dewfall daisy.
When she kissed, it was ripe, tender as a plum.

Whose salt we scatter now;
silent, on incredulous earth.

GONE TO SEA

He used to lie and kiss me
afternoons;
while the ships passed, the grassy wind
went by the dunes.

Lie and plait me fancies,
wedding spells;
till the sea tingled
and nodded: bells.

O time's a sailor's story,
luck a fever ship
and love a loaded blanket —
mother, you never told me this.

O come and put me under,
put me under quick:
I feel the pangs, the splitting fangs,
the orphan kick.

He picked me like a boy thrift,
sang me like a rhyme;
he stamped his loins upon my own
and will not give my child a name.

ESTUARY

In the crook of land's arm
water sleeps: a girl but
for a filigree necklace of bird-call,
naked.

The sky's forget-me-not
and crowfoot.
Tail-lit, a plane cuts;
memorial, ruby.

Over the viaduct
trains go home;
into the sound of hills,
the thighs of time.

ANN'S LULLABY

O my boneless morsel with the snailhorn fingers
and tiny mother of pearl toenails
turn from this tearful eye-rubbed fury;
settle for woman s arms.

O my brave papoose in the scalloped shawl
ripe and snug as a half-shelled almond
kick your frantic last, lie leisurely . . .
drift, dream.

Like a seed blown from a dandelion clock
a soap bubble whispered from a pipe
in a cornflower sky that never breaks
triumphant as a blessing ride . . .

and when the dandelion hour's a dropped toy
the jaunty bubble touched and gone
dream yourself awake — a smell of milk
this earth, these arms about you.

FANCY WOMAN

There the shocker is, all tricked out
like a bloody maypole — should be stopped!
But she's broke and entered, like she did before —
and she's staying to see him off —
the brooch he gave our lass
winking between her scrubber's tits
— our lass that's trying to hold up there
moidered with mauling kids, white with tears —
while she's stood bold as a jay
— stiletto heels, blue rinse —
slung with that stinking polecat she swears is mink,
tarted up for the wake she won't get to.
Never a touch of black to save her shame,
wearing a ring too —
her eyes prodding our menfolk, her thighs smirking
"This is what he saw in me, this, this —
And did he give it up?"

SURVIVOR

The scarved donkeys
are away with the gipsy
and his coachman's
whip of a wand;
the carousel
of lilting nags
and grinning dragons
tarpaulin statues.
Stacked, a hundred
deck chairs freeze.

And still he goes,
lost summer's waif,
shoving the chipped yacht
his father gave him
doggedly across
the green deserted
paddling pool,
next year's wind
in his ragged sails,
an eager sun
on his shoulder.

GRAFFITI

They've changed. At our village halt,
inside the tin and glass shelter,
the mene, mene, tekel, upharsin's not
'I want to suck you off, meet me 6 p.m
up Jacob's Lane,' or, 'Man' United — crap'
(loopy capitals like trains jumping the rails
or pokerwork harsh as Punch's bludgeon)
but bawdy, touching things —
'I wuz into necrophilia till she split on me'
(flanked with a penis blithe as a stick of rock)
or — with line breaks exact as a poem's —
'I have felt A. Smith. Big lovely ones.'
And A. Smith, at home, with the folks out,
deep breathing for a mirror's delectation,
preening, watching her breasts ride —
told by excited schoolmates Anon had written
(upside down, so one was teased to read)
that public, pagan testimonial . . .
And would she split on him, that spry familiar?
Only with cleaving life, big lovely ones, yes, yes.

LAST RESORT

A forbidden, rickety pier
touting torn photos of Big Daddy.

Scarred dingies swashing at anchor.
Wingless gulls tucked into themselves.

The esplanade rain-measly.
White flags of faces at windows.

A haunch-splayed Alsatian retching,
brought to heel by a snorted leash.

A wind surfer half a mile out
capsizing his image, heaving up again.

Shoe boxes jamming a litter bin.
A varicose waitress trashing a fag.

Waves limp as grey mortar
mooching in regardless, flopped back.

RIVIERA

Noon's a deck chair.
Sea a snoozy purr.
Round with his hypo
the sun shoots
dreams, golden comas.

Night risks a star.
Sea's a lazy paw.
The moon tiptoes
on high heeled shoes
over the sun's pink pyjamas.

BOARDSAILOR

A touch heroic, really
the way you straddle
that spare plank;
pick up a standard
from watery nothing,
drive it at blue —
your craft fizzing
the wave tops
thirsty as a fuse.

Now you're a painted feather
scudding half the bay;
a butterfly paused to graze
its huge, delighted flower —
and here, just off the island,
there's your silhouette, we watch
the fond wind round you out,
complete you, as the radiant thought
of a lover, a breast.

TUBE TRAVELLERS

The younger's halfcaste: melon-skinned;
three rings (one blue) on her left hand;
plus a brace of necklaces, loose-looped —
smiles quick as a lighthouse, comes on
like a Ghanese fishing boat gaudy for land.

The other's straight black, sober —
her coat mahogany, a Gospel hangover . . .
the massive soul of female choirs launched
from white walled missions decades since —
(she has a cold, dabs her wide nose).

Their Afrocuts bell out like twins,
but they are mother and daughter —
seas away from the Gold Coast beaches
that buffed their bare feet
— the purple banana buds and splay-eyed hammerhead sharks —
yet whose surf rides their vowelled Ashanti
bold as the paddle thrash that spoke their fathers, coming in.

DIPPER

That hole behind the waterfall,
that hole in his brood's belly,
is a blasting, incessant pain in the head
to stop which he'll do anything.
See him skindive, rock after rock —
there, stooped to the toppling swirl,
he'll be walking his underwater miracle,
shifting the mazy, roaring bottom
for snail dollop, beetle gut —
even now, when April snow
has the astonished beck
shrill as a tube train.
And there — mouthful after flying mouthful —
watch him hurl again, mad as a dambuster,
through the flak tornado,
the fall's endless avalanche . . .
out again to dance that snow-mossed rock,
dance with the life-span bawling in his head,
the compulsive salivating void,
the hole in all their belly.

TENEMENT

The yard offers
fireweed   skeletons
a smashed milk bottle
half bricks

a broken pane
stopped with cardboard
stencils
the greasy air

on a step
a mulatto kid
with a snail-crawled nose
chews orange peel

the bluebottle's
back on the sill
thrashing

the stairs sicken

kicked-in   beercans
rinds of silver paper
fagpulp

an old man
smelling of bacon fat

impasto cockroach
still on his boot

slumps
over a furrowed grate

in a back room
open for love
a woman
has just made

tonight's headlines

silently

in blood

SWISS COTTAGE

Lisbeth and Harry
my aunt and uncle
kept house together
thirty years.

She heard
a voice from heaven
calling "My Child"
and went to God
(incidentally acquiring
a sweetshop).

He caught
a whiff of steam
from sidings
and went footplate
(on the way inhaling
Socialism).

Thereafter
it was Russia the Antichrist
foretold in Revelations
but powerless
to spite the Chosen;

Capitalism the Antichrist
— with the accent on 'pit' —
falling to Russia
the Saviour
foretold in Marx . . .

aspirin kisses
china tea
with a confidante
of like persuasion
and a passing
that left the air
with a snowflake's
frail gentility

clammy oilrags
matey beer
retirement to
brute arthritis
and a finish
that had something to do
with the liver,
what else.

Harry and Lisbeth,
brother and sister,
living in time . . .
leaving me
their cuckoo-clock.

RAINFOREST CHILD

Monday my mother's groan was me.
The hut simmered, women's palaver.
They stroked my male inch with a palm leaf.
Outside, my grandmother smoked.

Tuesday my father let me touch his blowpipe.
I watched him spit monkeys
out of high, glittering leaves.
We smelled hot flesh, sucked the bones.

Wednesday I came to woman.
We drank palm wine brewed in a slit trunk.
Rain fell: a bouncy cliff.
I woke the leaping pool of her belly.

Thursday the sun roared, out of a golden mane.
I strode in chiefs amulets, wore kingfisher plumes.
Mosquitoes blew tiny conches,
swore to honour me, blood brothers.

Friday a guinea worm lolled out of my leg.
They wound it round a strong twig, slowly,
to catch it, fetch it whole.
The god was mine; nothing broke.

Saturday I trod on a mamba's whip;
my body swam with bad magic.
the juju man brought a skin of snake-teeth,
hung it on a bough.

Sunday my enemies wore dancing masks.
Drums told my death. Beyond the trees
I met my great grandfather, his face
like mine smiling out of smoke.

PARK FAMILIAR

Sometimes there'd be sparrows:
one eye on you, one on the bread;
trying to rush, grab,
in a single take-off.

Others you'd just sit (perhaps
time would straighten
out of its vain dropsy,
your belly-bulge at last evaporate) . . .

or move off determinedly anonymous;
step stilted as a metronome,
clothes as
heavily   correct.

You may have come for swans
— sudden, stencilled in lamp-velvet —
what's certain is
you came often, at night mostly.

For air maybe (one of those dusk folk
with pipes set like masthead lights)
who don't like dogs, who float around
happy with themselves . . .

or catharsis, walking off
a day's humiliations, its bossy rancid debts;
tracing a magic circle,
resolving for tomorrow . . .

or in a rapist dream of young flesh
(overtaken at 2 a.m.
by sobbing loins, the jerked reminder
of an empty place).

Or so I speculate: in your decade
the adolescent, with life to run —
but now, given that hindsight edge,
old, near enough to wonder

— so powerfully does your image lean
out of inbuilt consistent shadow —
if you are what I might have been —
or even, am.

CHURCHYARD STROLL

I lift a sunlit latch, go to meet them:
residents, features, grass.

A pink dove folds into an elm.
A birch casts a thousand thready
anchors on the blue.
Mauve crocuses have loosened out.
In the square the minute hand
of the clock is a shaft of gold.

A bell striking the first quarter
suddenly is jammed, swiped across
by jets, the sky huge with their splitting.
The sun's scuttled; I shiver, walk on
past the wired carbon paper glaze
of stained glass windows, the tiny stall
of wooden crosses stuck with cloth poppies,
the barred wheel of the modish Saxon cross
to an eighteenth century headstone,
its flatfish urn, holes for eyes,
swimming vainly upwards.
Underfoot, a slab is mumbling in red sandstone
about its slack tenant
a surgeon apparently —
the staunch chisel strokes that spoke for him
long since stuttered into moss.

The dove claps out of its elm;
I am here with the clock's broken arrow,
my lancet shadow on the grass.

MAINSTREET HOTEL

Outside, bald as a boiled sweet,
sodium lighting freezes the scuffed leaves.
Small hour traffic late home from the coast
waspishly volleys, fades.
The bedside table's purest chipboard,
the cold water blandly tepid;
pull the light cord, it chimes — twice.
It's three a.m. That traffic won't give up.
My back's cold. I plug it with the duvet,
take a bent ear out of the pillow, smooth it.
Front steps, a man from Minnesota's
telling the manager go sack himself.
A white coach marked 'Continental Tours'
simmers and flickers by the entrance, while Elmer
— young Elmer — cuts back for Momma's Turkish wrap.
Suddenly she's out of bed, sure it's a flea,
we scour everything, check check
like a Chinese laundry after a lost button.
Someone down the corridor starts hammering
a nail out of a shoe — into my waiting head;
someone else is actually snoring —
an asthmatic hoover in a chambermaid's bad dream.
Then crisp, insane as a guillotine, silence.
I mute my climax so's not to rouse
the man next door, who with equal charity
is quietly strangling his wife.

DEAR _____

We came to study penguins, why they're unafraid.
In that island restaurant of cold beaches,
among walrus colonels and duchessy seals,
they were like a school for head waiters, those birds —
with their coat tail flippers, white fronts.
Then my father had the stroke. If he's still alive
when you get here — if you do — he knows
what he wants to say but it comes out scrambled
(he'll get angry, stab with his stick, hot eyes.)
Between nursing, I stumbled on with research.
Then the seaplane with our two months ration
didn't show; the radio snapped into gibberish:
babble, bawl, propaganda, orders.
And four days later, the men:
that cavalier of a yachtsman who was cockleshelling the world
and had been blown into a fanged bay,
and the partisan with the bullet-scorched sleeve
who'd outfoxed — so far — the sniff of their patrols.
Both desperate with hunger, fatigue.
We took them in. Then the blizzard pounced:
blocking our windows, sandbagging us in.
Now we have two days food, no fuel.
Should they get here first, after the thaw
has liquified our clumped relics,
they will find this letter; sneering, tear it up.
Should it be you though . . .
The men here want to give me a child.
I am to choose.

COMEDIAN

This flash wagtail of a fellow tripping
his flippant shallows or feather-witted
tiptoeing lawns with an eccentric tail
like a smoker's finger flicking ash —
this fop fool that so prettily pursues
nothing but his own sweet vanity, it seems —
mark him.

No epicure more formidably relishes
his métier, instinctive food.
Not one dodge of the incessant game,
the gnat-dazzle that excites the stream,
but he can emulate, confirm and kill
in a brusque, beaked-lightning aside.

Mark him. Among those humours that appear
outlandish, scrawled upon the sheeted air,
among those quirkish characters that vindicate the stroke,
one could be ominously relevant —
most sincerely, yours.

THE PRICE

That field in the shadowy bloom of its seedheads,
moon daisies, clip-on moths,
somehow it stayed uncut.
Maybe the farmer died that year,
left its high estate to its natural span.
Whatever, it was good to see:
a wind-touched movement building all of summer
in its grass and grace.
Those splintery minarets of fescue,
rosy swags of sorrel!
What of his Freisians then, their winter feed?
Could they survive on such aesthetic whimsy'?
They'd need to. Someone pays the price for beauty:
why not a gum-chewing layabout now and then?

LISA

Peal, pizzicato — that's water hitting
a dip between moss-shawled stones.
A marigold sun, and where the gnats fidget
a ripple of trees, silk screen printed.

Kids and puppies playing on the bank
are biting gentle horseshoes out of each other.
In a driftwood alcove there's a tossed coke tin,
the crushed hauberk of a crayfish shell.

Sunlight trembles, rope-ladders a trunk.
Trout hover, fins ticking.
Mayfly tandems drift, split.
A lapwing falls on its own shadow.

The beck goes into a rain-game of quoits
And by the looped lifebelt post,
hand-punishingly carved in oak:
I married Lisa May First '78.

BETWEEN SEA AND GRASS

Old men,
clock-punched morning faces
now exempt, free

down by the pier ribbing each other
— close-moored boats
in a sly commotion of wavelets

or on seats round the bowling green
surprised by the odd dark velvet butterfly
left over from autumn's conjuring sleeve

old men, finishing their time
between sea and grass,
equably.

HERE

Here's a mare
parrying poniard flies
with an easy, lazy tail.

Swallows chatting
like barber's scissors
over the thatched roof

and three poplars:
giraffes lipping
a blue endless

leaf of sky

SWOT

They pinch my bag
rip the strap off
stuff it with Stink Horn
leave it in the shower

throw pumps at me
call me "Crab Eyes"
tie my legs together
roll me down the bank.

I told the form master once.
They took my rough book
wrote GRASS all over
in green felt tip.

It's not my fault
I'm good at maths
and don't like a hard ball.

I know I'm rather
absent-minded
and sometimes
don't hear the bell

I know I'm
a bit eccentric
and sometimes
chatter on like a kid

but when I'm happy
my time's not theirs
but the kind
clouds have, in the summer.

I'd like to leave,
live on an island;
scoff melons
and coconut scoop —

do calculus
with my feet up,
ride elephant turtles
down to the sea.

DIESEL DRIVER

A six foot windscreen and a bench of gadgets,
easy as wafting a kid's three wheeler.
Left lever off and let her gather,
feel her pull, strong, her rhythm settle,
check with wristed time, make the straight, faster —
Gobowen, Ruabon, Wrexham, Chester.

Flush a thatch of fantails, a hawk from hover,
send a linesmen skittling for banked cover,
make the butterfly-tossed bay willow rustle,
the corn-set poppies flinch and wrestle —
give an extra toot if you see your sister —
Gobowen, Ruabon, Wrexham, Chester.

Far off those lines must surely meet —
like looking up the straddled legs of a giant.
They never do. Now it's curve, meander,
slack off a bit, watch points.
Then the first houses, a tightening cluster —
Gobowen, Ruabon. Wrexham, Chester.

Wail for slow down, shush to a stop,
doors clacked open, porters' hustle.
'Trust The Lord With All Your Heart' on placard.
Llangollen coracles, trolleys tipped,
a last sweaty passenger in a swearing fluster —
Gobowen, Ruabon, Wrexham, Chester.

Then off again, hummed past the signal
— a thoughtful heron angling its red-white beak —
under a leapfrog come and go of bridges,
skirting the old sandpit, the men fishing,
round where the woods lean over, the jackdaws muster —
Gobowen, Ruabon, Wrexham, Chester.

Trim as a trout in a Sunday suit,
snug as a grape in a Guernsey greenhouse,
who's to sigh for the steamy past?
No more gritty eyes, blown caps, cracked faces —
not even an oil-tarred shirt, a footplate blister —
Gobowen, Ruabon, Wrexham, Chester.

CLEARING THE ATTIC

We finished yesterday. And now
Geoffrey Holloway aged three
comes into the living room, looks across
out of an oval frame with glass gone,
but only slightly flyspecked.

Some pro whose bones untied long since
discovered him, like every other —
dressed up for keeps by a doting aunt —
in one of those cream, embroidered smocks
the genteel poor seemed to cherish then.

He sits at table, chin on pudgy hand
(the tucks in the palm neatly blacker).
You can see maternal fingers behind that hair,
sluicing suds off, while he grizzles;
but it's come up clean as larch needles.

The sun's finger chooses his lip.
He looks at me, absurdly vital.
But years have smashed reflection;
I cannot see myself in him —
only touch a paper sleeve.

DRUNK

Your joy was in that bottle. Now it's gone.
The walls are swimming — and the seasick floor.
Where will it end'? Legless, in the john?

No God-flung shoulder to cry on.
No magic carpet to lift you any more.
Your pride was in that bottle. Now it's gone.

No friend to crawl to, no bank to con,
no way that isn't caught in a swing door.
Where did it start'? Legless, in the john?

Your faith was in that bottle. Now it's gone.
Down the endless hatch. And what's the score?
One more for the road — to oblivion.

Oh you were tasty once, tough as Napoleon's baton.
But you'd joined for keeps, you lost the war.
Where must it end? Legless, in the john?

Ants trickling your belly, rats locked on.
Snakepit horrors you thought nevermore.
Your love was in that bottle. Now she's gone.
And you? Legless, in the john.

THE GAFFERS

Fine afternoons the gaffers surface,
sitting the green as they've always done

ingrained with the benches,
cracking on with cronies

about the footloose days when they smoked paper
left coins for the express to flatten

stole the bobby's gloves
untethered the prize bull . . .

calmly aghast at old iniquities
that never seem to die

yet shameless about their own near-dotage,
the mould in their cheesy brains.

Weather's into them: the jab and nag
of arthritis in their heavy bones

and often silence, as if their thoughts
were too alike to waste on speech.

Dusk falls, gold bulrush heads
begin to quiver in the beck;

cocooned in the mist that's apt
to travel with them they unstiffen

start for home.

SENIOR CITIZEN

Stocktaking, dawdling on:
the faint clench of arthritis
round the hand, the faint stoop
and blossoming paunch . . .
everything faint.

Things kept going to keep one going:
a few friends, dutifully close,
a shrub or two to tidy up.
dab at the crossword,
stroll, pint.

Some pleasures: to catnap an afternoon:
watch from an upstairs window
the lilt of breasts;
occasionally checkmate
a bright nephew.

And worries, tactless elbows —
will the handrail survive one's weight:
dare one still drive at night;
what of the heart
if lips go blue . . .
Amnesia, apathy, incontinence
— the real markers —
not obtrusive yet.
Nor the last dream — of the open boat,
lost oars, black approaches.

STROKE

She must have had it
putting her stockings on

they're still furled
round her ankles

and she half-lying
in an armchair

head to one side
like a fallen nestling

she can move one leg
the other, well,
it's a shiny pole

all down one side it's gone

that arm stuck across her chest

but she can answer

monosyllables drop
from the squint in her mouth
like pebbles

her lids are shut like cat flaps
eyebrows ginger still

strange how one never noticed that
when she was high-stepping off
to her bridge parties

the grandson who found her
knocked us up
like an Alamein barrage

we thought it was Ellen fooling
but by then he was battering
next door

poor kid to come on this
looked as if he'd never seen
a shaving stick

teeth on the mat

next door's kitten
peeping round a bed leg

after hide and seek

not this stiff-lapped
stranger

MONITORS

Across the ward green biros of monitors
compete for Sister's eye:
one switchbacked daft as the Road Runner,
the other rippling evenly: a child's drawing of waves.
My locker's a surreal tip:
GET WELL cards from the kids, boldly misspelt
(earwigs, dogs, caterpillars wreathing
and peering round the capital Ls)
next to a howl of pinks, the peripatetic urinal.
When they came to see me the day after
I splurged into cliché: "Thank God you're here!"
Blaspheming, slobbering my well-kept image,
letting myself disgracefully (but thankfully) down.
They are thinning my blood with rat poison;
the syringe driver at my wrist confirms it.
Twelve hours, it will whine from nowhere,
a mosquito-bleep, wanting a refill, more.
When I told him I felt something there —
more than a twinge at the top of the testing breath —
the dapper auburn Consultant checked,
reading the spoor of his stethoscope round nipples, chest.
"Ay, there's the pleural rub, gentlemen" —
leaving his white smocked gaggle to hear it too.
They gave me morphia that night, from the zonker's trolley;
its wash-leather wiped me clean;
I shone like a new window, for six hours.
That one by the door came in yesterday,
ruckling like someone spading up snow on gravel,
coughing from clinker-grey to beetroot.
They clapped a respirator on him, against those pillows
he's beaky as a puffin in a chalk niche —
that is, when he doesn't throw it away
to hiss like a gas leak.
Sometimes they screen us off, for no apparent reason —
then show us it: the empty bed.
They tell me the pain will go. Will it? Will it?
Their hands, their optimistic hands.

AN ESSAY ON THE SHAKING PALSY
(James Parkinson 1817)

Parkinson my mother never met. But he knew
all about her: the drool, the stuttery gait,
cement-like face and fist that trembled;
thumb and finger incessantly twiddling
as if trying to open an invisible door.

While she could still walk I'd let her lead me
— backwards, the hands in mine
head-nuzzling like hungry cats.
'The Lancers' we liked to call it,
that dance she loved as a girl.

Doll-like, hunched, was the way she went;
black hair still glossily intact
but on her cheek a glaring flush;
made up for Death like it was Christmas
and he some famished child-cripple.

Do the kept complain? She didn't, ever.
But if she had, committed
sawbones that he was,
Parkinson, his pen flowing symptoms,
doubtless would have logged it

with the same curious dispassion
he gave to describing fossils
— his other love —
or the sometimes uneven bubbling
of his own, rented pulse.

BLIND DATE

Seeing by touch, you manage, just;
touring the cottage doing your 'little jobs',
pleased you can still do them, almost well.

That was the mail, wasn't it, hitting the mat.
Next door will read it, if she's in later.
Doubtless a few holiday ads among it.

Acapulco, Biarritz, Costa Del Sol . . .
the names will tease your ear
but you won't complain of what you're missing —

rather cap the lack with reminiscence
of your own favourite spots, times —
so vividly your compensation's our bonus.

Life's already cut you off enough —
I'd like to think you'd guarantees
against incurring further niceties

but prophylactics don't seem mandatory;
the glass you smashed last week
(you thought you'd scoured it all up)

sharpens its nasty glitter on the floor;
any morning now you could wake up
feeling for a noise — and trip over

the chunk of home you call your 'good eyes',
its breath unharnessed, at the door.

CROSS MY HEART

and hope to live. There's a clot somewhere,
drifting like a floe.

Something hardening to keep me here —
on appro?

That geezer four beds down is snoring
like a rogue pneumatic drill;

sounds like someone slipped a cosh
into his anti-coag pill.

Tuesday it was Florrie Nightingale I dreamt:
the Tenth Muse, wheeling a commode . . .

bodywork choicest Chippendale;
and the inset, Spode.

Tonight maybe Dracula, menthol fresh,
fangs meeting with a maddened clack;

casing a forest of swabbed forearms
for a sip of vintage haemophiliac.

I've saved my nectarine for three a.m.;
when the sleeper's done.

Last night she ordered me to take it early.
I told her shove it. Strangely, won.

Him that's up scuffs from the Day Room,
tells the dripsters we're three goals down

(some of them are so infused
it's a miracle they don't drown).

Bed, board, drugs provided —
why don't I smuggle the missus in;

(shouldn't be all that hard, rearranged
in a laundry bin).

Next Consultant's Round will they
nail us to our bed rests, to look neater —

or bash us with meditation-therapy
one hundred OMs from the Bhagavad-gita?

Cross my heart and tell a lie.
Nobody has time to die.

SALT 'N VINEGAR

I may not be much these days,
can't hold up like I did.
Forget my keys,
burn the toast.
But the girl in the chippie likes me
— and that's a fact.

Her eyes seem to soften
when I come in
and glow a bit.
It may he only quick
as a traffic light
but it doesn't feel like that.

Maybe she's just happy,
there's a few that way.
Maybe she's fond of old folks,
there's someone at home like me.
Or she could be the same with everyone . . .
But I don't know.

I look at her tiny earrings,
her spotless cap, her grin.
And she doesn't have
to flash me the wink
to say there's one or two
extra in.

And if I'm slow one day
with the coppers,
fumble opening my bag
before I'm halfway through
she'll be giving a hand
— not too obvious though.

When I don't go in does she notice,
say "My young man missed today"?
No matter. When I do it's same as always,
right as a cracker on Christmas Day.
Salt 'n Vinegar? Life I call it.
And that's a fact.

STILL LIFE

Last night again the dream: running
barefoot over moonfire grass.
Tonight as usual: the vice of breath
that won't end it, has you scraping through
matted inches, trying to suppress
the tickle, the cough of knives
that cuts to retching, choking.

Your glasses scowl from the bedside table,
crab-like, with black malicious claws;
by the commode your precious Zimmer's
a dusty stiff legged souvenir.
How long can you keep on
to nowhere, that endless cave . . .
how much do you want to, even?

Morphia? That lovely thorn
with its flower of respite's not prescribed
— respiration would be depressed.
So you have to lie and sweat them out
— chewing them like a dolt a pencil —
the rancid, restless hours,
the same useless questions.

Can you expect love? Did you give enough?
This month will they come again,
the gifted friends, flesh of your pillow?
Or are they gone for ever, like silver fish —
down cracks, under floorboards of excuse?

How long can you live like this,
snarled up with naff familiars:
the jellyfish wad of phlegm in the mug,
the lamplit slug on the path that never moves,
this rain whispering all the cripples in the world?

A SHEAF OF FLOWERS

ALDER

Remembering her Winter choice
— that obdurate black bombasine —
you'd think coquetry
the last shift
this gawky puritan
would approve.

But February
must have spiced her pulses —
here she rides, teasing the dimpled beck
with catkin earrings, like red snowdrops.

ALLOTMENTS: FEBRUARY

Bits of gale-ripped fence
flat as duckboards

a sunflower stump
in pot-shaped soil

in the borders
crocuses gaping

someone snapping off
last year's canes

trash flaunting
a broadsword of flame

wispy twigs
of sycamore

on the topmost
a thrush boasting

a shrew stiffened
round its grin

the child insisting
on burial.

APRIL DUSK

Tiles
are warm
with remembered
sun.

I burn sticks;
their grey
blowy smoke
tangs my hair.

Cherry petals
haunt the grass
like old
love letters.

A star
is coming
through the air —

like a new one.

ANTI-NUCLEAR DEMO

Spectators leave us like another river.
Only time knows which course is right:
theirs, or ours that ends here,
in this tired, protesting square.

Past police chewing bored chinstraps,
gaggles of stalled, blaring cars,
natives waiting for buses, tourists waiting for us,
we have dribbled through . . .
a motley straggle, plutonium in our eyelets,
seesaw children asleep on our backs,
jerking cardboard banners, shouting in tatty unison.

Here in the square the earth is with us,
though sand lines its cracks at our feet
and no ostrich-plumy fountains sway —
only the Tannoy . . .
from a platform flanked with stone lions
faith for the faithful, tiny spokeswomen
with dark glasses like pennies on their eyes.

ATISHOO ATISHOO

I have this dream, see.
I'm walking barefoot, a lake of ice,
when this skyscraper office block
(cigarette-lighter type)
keels over, falls
right through me.

No one's hurt. It's only me
stuck out at this crazy right angle
like some suckered cat burglar
or window cleaner —
me, a soundproof sky,
and at my feet — intact —
the office block,
looking as if they were all
on telly, as if they didn't know
it had all — the world — gone
suddenly flat on them.

My right foot's in that typist's mouth
but she doesn't take out her fag.
My left's on the boss's tonsure —
slip, I'd smack
into that gape of waste bin.

So, no move.
So, I'm here till zero
(my heart bashing, chipping
my granite ears)

or

hell, someone opening a window.

AUBADE

You must have gone while I slept
(if you were ever there).
Whispered your clothes on,
left like a ghost.
And now it's dawn again,
thinning the curtains,
and time of course
— black minutes flashed
from a perspex clock,
a scrambled duvet,
rough dent in a pillow —
time that while
we were building love
was maybe a chink somewhere,
video taping.
And was it time then that hoicked you
out of my life, an agent briefed
for the next unkind assignment?

Love now, tomorrow's fiction.
A theme from Omar, all this way.
Meanwhile, world's back, the ache of your absence.
Bluetits are jabbing at putty outside.
So does their insistent morse mean anything?
Only that bluetits need feeding, no doubt.
As does time. And this guest billeted on me
who seems to lounge about cleaning his gun all day,
waiting — so I understand — for a bleep
that will pay him, give him the right to move.

FAMILY FUNERAL

Summoned from hillside farms and lawny mansions,
villas, semis a skein of motorways apart,
why do we gather with our drained faces,
false teeth hung out to dry,
funny guts, dubious hips,
blood pressure, bald bits,
to stand about this blotchy landslipped
stone, these marble chips?

To watch while the youngest adolescent
pours white smoke in the corner of a tomb
rank with stale bones and proxy mentions —
dead of two wars and time's impatience?
To trail in convoy to someone's house,
eat ham and cake, ask each other
where the children are, the grandchildren
(whose names we'll have mislaid once more
when the next contender's ripe for ritual)?

No need to track down years for an answer.
This dropped dust, our so-and-so that was
— bitchy, erratic, promiscuous for sure —
never once locked her face against us,
never refused to take us in —
however scapegrace, thankless, short.

Sap of that same prehensile root
how dare we now deny her houseroom,
due part in this scrolled earth
its clannish, fecund story?

BATHROOM FLIES

These small
how many explorers

caught in trackless
enamel canyons

drowned in toppled
sudden marshes

gone missing
along shelving docks

between skyscraper shaving stick
and soap barge

these innocent
jump jetting

in circles
inches away

as if they lassoed safety
by simply describing it

these wanton
skidding off

the saving wafer
of toilet roll

coquettes
playing with life

as if it were slapstick
some outsize joke

what can we make of them
that only end

like the scrawl
of a child's pencil

pressed hard

that suddenly snaps.

BEACH-HEAD

Waves come sizzling in, throaty, drink themselves back.
A couple of kite duellists mob the sky,
slice it with loops, power dives, bizarre calligraphy.
A girl clops by on a white horse, streamy hair
repeating the lilt of its tail.
A red setter moustached with a stick
prances, flounces, tempting its master to attack.

Shut the poetic door, they're still there —
the spar of the lost yacht idling home between troughs;
the donkey shadow traipsing its stint of shore;
hard laughter of gulls, yellow beaks
ripping at crumpled bags blown off the pier.

DEAR SECOND BED DOWN

may I, as Consultant in the case,
spare a precious second or so
to say what a pleasure it is
finally to allow you Graduation Status.
Your performance in all departments of the cure
has been nothing short of magnificent.
You have responded to the chemotherapy
superbly, as we hoped you would.
Wisp by wisp your hair is returning.
You have dieted, visualised, vindicated
our somewhat tentative hormone programme.
Your blood is beginning to redden up;
your X-rays are stunningly clear.

It is with God's own pleasure I hang
this medal round your neck.

Now go and die of something else.

COMEBACK

They must be all out there — of those alive anyway.
Bookings have been sensational. "Scarbo. Scarbo!"
they're bawling my name, the auditorium's seething.
Shortly they'll start to stamp their feet. And it will come:
"Oh why are we waiting . . . ?"

Dolts. They're thirty years back, in the sway
of an ikon, a ghost in a glistening topper
who has deigned to indulge them for an hour
in his spotlit, enchanted playroom . . .
who will snap his fingers into flame,
whisk a rose from behind an ear, loose a flurry
of doves with gold chains round their necks,
pack a busty girl into a sarcophagus,
halve, heal, in a few breathless minutes
have her back smiling, all tights and spitting sequins
to wave to them, wave their eyes back to his genius.

Scarbo, The Great Scarbo. Is this him —
this seamy dinner-jacketed potato
sweating behind the curtain now?

Why did I let myself be flattered back?

Or am I dreaming, is this a hilarious con,
will some grinning "This Is Your Life" clown
erupt from the wings, lush portfolio under his arm,
and the boards wince, the flats sprout familiars:
my schoolgirl sweetheart, a Mormon uncle,
the Staff Sergeant who set me up with that nickname
a tiddly impresario they thought might tickle memory,
my drooling granny, some one else on a stick?

No such elaborate getout. I'm here like I was,
to do my act, before a curtain still smeary
with matted fagsmoke and stale booze smells —
here with the quaking butterflies I thought blown away
for ever, with the dust from my doll's house props.

Prospero, Mephistopheles, Zeus — whoever's up there
in the staring gods tonight, defeat's one trick I can't take.
Don't refuse me your wrinkled magician's hands, wands.
Stand by our covenant. Put me in debt to honour;
don't let me weasel out down the back stairs.
Make me go on in the central starch of the spotlight
then as the clapping sputters out grant me
one last stupendous boon.
Let them see me, then heypresto! see me go,
evaporate into immortalised thin air
in a bang of smoke, a tingling drumroll crescendo —
Scarbo The Incomparable, his final total miracle.

But who are these, these hulking yobs dressed up as stage hands
swearing, clumping about, knocking down the flats to shove it on,
this rusty iron trampoline?

What would I want with an iron trampoline?

The curtain begins to yawn.

A SHEAF OF FLOWERS

One side's gone. I'm on your good one.
I put a finger in at your dry fist.
It sucks me, a child at the nipple.
I want more. I won't get it.

Left side of the bed, waving
a sheaf of flowers, she's trying
to raise your eyes.
"Daffs from our garden — look!"

And now she's at you with kisses —
such as the tall daughter with her
may have sprung from
tangled decades gone.

Around, the block's at its business.
A cook cries over onions,
a porter's out for a drag.
Relatives are told to bring clothes in.

Pneumonia. The stroke. Then gangrene.
To stop you dying quicker, they docked your leg.
You moan when they turn you;
you've that much left.

You used to fell race with a fox's flair.
Supple young swam from your eager mating.
But the red man in your blood's tired;
dries distant, heavy.

Time for earth now. The last lap:
stillness under a tree root —
and a quieter kin than daffs .
primrose, windflower.

OLD MAN

Hairs rush out of his nose and ears
nails jut like windshields

he gabbles confidently
but names tease him like magician's cards

bluetits are exploding round
the red sock beyond his sill

he looks through them
like a meths drunk

an elder brother's
still hiding his clobber

he scrabbles hours under furniture
for things he had perfectly minutes before

has to crane to hear — and what comes through
is rhymed rhubarb

someone like his old headmaster
is shoving him along a corridor
by the back of his neck

each shuffling step pushes
his head down further

like a drunk's under a tap

his body is beginning to slump
on the iron hook of his neck

he can see himself falling into the fire

dead meat

if it were only that

PENULTIMATE

To look at a flower as if it were a boot sole;
have a mind of pitted gorgonzola
that forgets even its own age

to be tar-handed, ramshackle —
take a quarter of an hour
squirming into your socks

to treble-lock the present
swaddle the future with insurance
feel breath freeze at a footstep

to wait for some flush hospital to take you in,
patch you out. To host torturers,
pray for the garrotte . . .

to look well, pass it off
— corruption's quiet shambles —
to be old.

PROGRESS

To dream in the apricot nursery of childhood,
green sunlight whispering through the blinds.
Teddy, your real brother,
sat up immortal on his miles of sofa;
Mummy's kiss the fairy tale guarantee.

To doze in the glaze of middle life .
the kids packed off and earning,
roses better than next door's,
the future lagged, the wife on tap,
early retirement only a slippered foot away.

To wake in the gutted bungalow of age,
the smash of cold after the gulping flame,
the stench, everything gone but a steel
mirror where you live with singed eyelids,
never to sleep again.

THE ELECT

They say he does it in one loop
his scalpel dainty as a fruit —
pat as peeling an apple.

I am ready, precisely schooled.
Chanting, approving hands
have led me on.
I know what I shall see:
the towels whiter than eggskin,
the herbal styptics,
The Book open at the still tongue of wisdom,
my brethren in the gallery

then my uncle the surgeon, vivid as cirrus
the scattering of his white hairs,
and in his gentle voice
the confidence of empathy.

Seven days, the healing is complete.
You walk free, in the franchise
of the brethren, born again in the tribal cut,
that manly shedding.

But what is this new, airless room?
And these strangers: this needle of a man
with the lisping, thin voice,
the tongueless black attendants?

You have sung well my child, he says.
Your voice has colonised the spandrels of eternity
chaster than one of His own doves.
You are His favourite. His and mine.
Before that voice dies into fleshy manhood
we must strike for purity.
It is not of course for my humility to say
if the thrill of remembered trebles
or the scream of agony endured for Him
he will most adore . . .

his hand is on me, under my cloak,
at my pouch, he tries
the soft ovals of our joy
adept as a nest robber

his slaves clot into shadow round me

he will do it with his eyes

the cold blue stone axe of his eyes.

FIREWORKS ON THE REC

Sue was laced around Dad's neck;
when the first rocket spilt its stars
she went "Ah" and stretched out for a handful;
you could see them in her big eyes.
She cried when the mine went off
— thunder, a van over a cattle grid —
so sudden even I blinked and Rob was so excited
he machine-gunned a fireman.
Then it was Roman Candles lobbing peacock's eyes,
more rockets, swooshing and popping —
stars like forget-me-nots, on stalks.
Sue had settled down by then, was scoffing
a hot dog — "All down your coat," Mum said.
After that they did what the tannoy called
a waterfall, real splashes where it landed,
then the set piece: between a tank
and what Grandad said was an S.P gun
(he was a Desert Rat in World War Two).
In the end they knocked each other out. Super.
And it was up at last, like it always is:
'GOOD NIGHT', in gynormous letters . . .
fading, bit by bit.
So we moved to the bommie, they'd lit it already,
it was great: a red wigwam.
Rob and his mates were dancing round it,
clapping their mouths into Red Indian cries,
flames on their faces like warpaint.
Till the roof-pole toppled, what was left of the guy
fell over into a smelly, smoky tyre.
And Sue began to twine. "Too much excitement,"
Mum said,
"About time we all went home."
It wasn't till we got there I found
my toes were cold, had been all the time.

LONG MEG AND HER DAUGHTERS

I've skimmed what bumph there is, of course:
stuff about barrow markers, Druidic worship,
a witch's curse turning red stones to blood.
One thing's for sure though: this is no accident,
no outcropped quirk, neolithic folly.
Something's about here that rounds off an era.
Long Meg for instance, what's she?
The ghost of a sarcophagus somewhere else?
A bumptious, home-compelling lingam?
A prod of belly with matriarchal slit beneath?
And the entourage, what's that? A clan? A coven?

Speculating, I go walkabout.
A sentinel ash glints in the wind,
its leaves a shoal of minnows.
A jet goes over, a snarling pipefish.
The smell of cowpats, glistening wheel hubs
mobbed by ginger dungflies, comes up strong
— after this surely the nose stays sceptical?
I look at webs trembling in sandstone pocks,
at grass happened in cracks, spiral patterns,
the scratched initials of some stray tourist,
at this, that. Suddenly find myself stood
in the middle of it all, my head a Bronze Age whirlpool;
still awed, by what doesn't matter.

'Long Meg And Her Daughters', is the name of a stone circle near Penrith.

LAST DAYS

Waking early is everything;
to catch through dawn's opening curtains,
slight but assured,
the burr of the first blackbird —

then down to a small breakfast,
out in the greenhouse to vet tomatoes,
check the netting over the strawberry patch,
feel apples firming on his tree.

Later perhaps he'll clip the hedge,
take some bubbly greatniece to school
do a bit of painting, change a fuse —
anything that's about, that needs an eye, hand.

And afternoons, fettle the bowling green
— with a spruce scurrying wagtail for mate
shave it like a royal barber, never
a cocky blade given the least quarter

while evenings are for sauntering the village
in a scent of pipe smoke and wall flowers,
dropping in for a pint and a rap of dominoes,
an easy, knowing joke round the table . .

or watching snooker, reminiscing —
the green baize a field of youth
where, plucked like balls from time's pockets,
they ran it: a cushioned, vanished world.

Today however inflection's altered —
this or that politician's yap
less crucial than the neighbour's kitten
stowed away under a parked car.

To be absorbed, comfortably unnoticed,
that long ambition's his now
lingering out a grateful span,
waiting for life to forget him.

LAZARUS

Two things about the old byre:
a broken window
and a martin's nest.
One the work of boys no doubt:
chucking stones from a mark
till no glass tinkled,
they could lounge off,
random feathers in the hair;
the other, art of a parent bird —
forked lightning whisper-shafting through
till dusk found its diving tail
in a pocket of drowsy mouths.
And was there a third thing?
Maybe a touch of myth:
the blind eye opened
on avid, certain grace.

A PROPER WOMAN

She won't take out her teeth.

My tongue rushing the drawbridge finds
a portcullis slammed on its ardour.

It's unromantic.

Me, I like a smack of the memento moris
— a grin at the bottom of a glass,
like a bit of reef or something
the octopus won't swallow —

but her, no.

She won't take out her rollers either,
says you can poke the fire
without unsettling the mantelpiece.

I daren't complain;
she'd put in central freezing.

DIET

"Nice job you have here, touring the Lakes."
I nod, tuck back into my social worker's car
— on the back seat liberal castoffs,
jigsaws, walking aids, a spare torch — thinking
from where I sit landscape means people, work.
My Lakeland polaroids aren't of lionpelt fells,
bandoliering sheepwalls, curlew tambourines,
dippers skimming becks that bask like blue snakes,
Wordsworthian ikons, Beatrix Potter dolls,
but what flanks them, that I have to meet:
the child of forty with the albino lock
grabbing my hands with pumice paws,
grunting, licking me as if I were coned ice cream;
the man whose pyjamas sag, whom cancer's bashing
random as a rookie spuds;
the man who yesterday drank death from a tarn,
letting its picture fill him, wall up the past;
the crone with scorched legs cuddling a stick fire
that one day she'll fall into,
frazzled wits burnt black as toast.

INMATES

They had been happening all summer, the impossible strangers,
whenever quiet sprang.
Though there was nothing to make a shadow
it would be there beneath the door —
spade-shaped, never moving
even when you opened the door.
And though the house was tight as a safe
— no pinhole treason anywhere —
even the faintest lull would hear that noise of a mouse,
slight but unmistakable, cracking its iron crumb.
And the spot of blood on the ceiling, wider,
dripping on closed, terrified eyes . . .
and when you snapped awake the crunch of steps
slow but definite, there on the gravel . . .
that broke off, always, mid-path.
Till the last night, the night before the fire.
You had sworn, remember, to rush, beat your panic.
Up from the gate you heard them coming . . .
flung from the bed, hurled to the window —
to find not gravel but snow, the shape of steps in it;
black, lost half-way.
And two days later, in a stench of gum boots,
among the charred, cold welter
the bones of a cat, a piece of door
— spade-shaped, not a singe on it . . .
blank as snow — but for a red speck.

GENERATIONS

I had been reading about death; between the lines
the Bren-gun titter of a gull.

The sky was grey hardboard.
There was snow outside, white concrete.
A few pollards scowled; squat, akimbo.

Mindless of my bitter drift
you stood against the upstairs window:
talking, in your light voice .
sloeberry eyes, tight kitten-face,
instant, leggy as a deer .

Over your shoulder suddenly that sky whirled,
ran like a deer's breath,
a wind through orchards:
teaming flakes that chased and gambolled,
head over heels, galore, like boys in clover.

I had been reading about death:
you between.

GIG

The last poem tucked beneath my chair
I sprawl on stage with the band, feet-tap
and watch myself in the trumpet's mouth
— tiny, hammocked, under a star-ceiling
terse as a Dutch interior.

He slants his horn to a coming sun,
eyes clamped on a long crescendo
holds me blazing in its tower —
then fades on a muezzin's cry . . .
sets light fingers on the valves of the heart;
steals me quietly, plays me like a lover.

And if salt earth between our touching
slide like a sweat bead, breaking out of time,
no matter; these notes will be others,
horned plenty in the lavish air;
always with hands beneath to lift and pour
inexhaustibly, here, there.

HOUSE ARREST

Walls are cardboard when you listen,
steel to the touch.
Scratch on them one day
it's erased the next.
Might as well scratch your crutch.

Softly. The guards have rubber soles.
And — they don't speak.
Tell the bug that;
in code of course.
It should sound unique.

Die? Don't you know? Against Orders.
But think: were you ever more than dumb?
Where's your Dad now? Your Mam?
What's with the wife? That safe job?
Somebody's doing it for you, chum.

Eight sharp. Guards get briefed.
Nine. Tin plate, spaced with nosh.
(Use your nails for knives;
they'll be long enough).
Ten. Before you wash

— viewed discreetly through a slit —
bowels may clock in.
Eleven. Re-education Time:
after me now, with the tape, repeat
'Thought Is the Original Sin.'

Hushaby then till the monitor-slot . . .
all night, breaking up the tomb,
laughter — at dreams, wet dreams.
Where are you now, my Shalimar queen?
Meet yourself, round the room.

Above the roof the heron barks.
Fishes wait to bleed.
Yesterday was like this.
A scream hangs in the bushes.
Where, who are you to plead?

ROE DEER: SUNSET

Far off there's only antlers
drifting the flood of summer grass

then bodies surface: a buck and two hinds;
sun-dipped, vermilion-swarthy.

Sniff, turn, challenge.
A bark staccato as a sentry's

and suddenly they're all leaping,
hurdling air with their curved going;

every few strides one higher,
as if bounced off a hidden trampoline

till effortless they vault the wall
into a dazzled wood.

OCTOBER

Lemony leaves of plum, gold
of cherry, long-stalked sycamore —
lazily invoking breezes
light enough to nod them off.

You cannot see the sunflower stems.
Like water lilies, balanced
on a day of limpid, royal blue,
heady nothings crown the air.

The woods are smoke-shadowy:
transposed, chromatic fantasies.
And we, sleepwalkers granted
a last magnetic opulence,

extravagantly drift, savour, before
the brave autumnal crayons drop —
and winter draws, with burnt matchsticks,
charcoal studies of despair.

SNOW ON GRUB STREET

So he's flipped, the attic genius —
either spilt his waste basket
or moulted, is scrapping
his past again
(doubtless to wow us once more
with the eternal virgin bit)

anyway down it comes:
a decade's clutter;
shoaling, swirling

chits, receipts, shreds
of old love letters,
fluffed images, bills, writs

— beneath the sudden skyslide,
in a white skullcap,
a robin (his next biographer of course)
tut-tutting about sorting truth from trash

when he isn't blasting off
like a mini flame thrower
at titfaced rivals.

TAKE-OVER

And the more he thought
the more it came to him,
monsters weren't fabulous any more —
not giants with tree trunks for clubs,
dragons dug in like flame throwers,
or gorgeous sirens way out and fraught
as Portuguese Men O'War —
but civilised, on the whole:
mild mannered men who suited fawn,
did their service with the Masons,
had a bit in oil,
adored their grandchildren,
saved black for funerals
and kept together.

TRAMP STEAMERS

To the boy throwing sticks for the wet dog,
scrawling giants on estuary sand,
reassurance, it was always coming,
edging deliberately in
until the prowed name, port of origin,
were eye-picked, indelibly there —
and tomorrow friendly, a gift of oranges
scented, brilliantly to hand . . .
and perfection, it was always going,
a wisp of smoke forbidden land
or any truck with measurable stock,
that was never seen as anything but itself,
would fray, fade, in its wilful time
imperiously slant again . . .
as ever, horizon-haunting, brief, inexhaustible.

TRAVELLING MAN

You've notched where you wanted, spluttered, sank.
Should be feeling relaxed now.

This hotel has telly in the bedrooms, yes?
And a bidet. Unusual, that.

But the wardrobe's a bit big for you really.
Like tonight, your heart, too much of it, bumping.

Will you be able to see round the bottle this month?
Send something home besides an excuse?

And how, where are the children these days?
Still in your wallet, matt-finish?

Any moment soon the woman will be saying
her son's pyjamas are like yours.

VACANT POSSESSION

I sit at her dressing table
still in pyjamas, one sleeve wet
from the weekend washing up;
soothing my frayed hair
with her silver backed brush.
An abandoned lipstick
puts out its tongue at me.
The taxi at the road's end,
rich the day it took her,
comes and goes, insolvent, fuming.
If this were Basho's book
it would be spring. Here
the cherry blossom's dirty frogspawn.
Soot felts my crevices.
I feel a fleck of tobacco on a tooth
— one of her rolled, forgotten Gauloises —
and remove it. It mars my finger.
All so very funny.
Last night I dreamt they sucked
my entrails through my nose.
Will tonight complete the embalming?
And where will she be now? Doing what?
In a motel somewhere applying
that warm smile
to some lounging crotch on a bar stool?
And a week ago she was warming her ears
at this record player; needling me
with Piaf the regrettable urchin.
Then, the row. But nothing we hadn't healed
a thousand times before.
And suddenly she's off like a snipe at a footstep.
Failure stings me like a neglected match.
I tick off my flaws, obtuseness.
Remember Tuesday, squeezing me helpless;
Thursday, that baleful vacuum.
Will she come back? Has she so much faith?
Something is dying in the North Sea.
The letter from nowhere could be due any moment.
I sit, watch myself in the mirror.
I am stitching my upper lip to a cushion.

WHERE FISH ARE, GOD IS

Another photo, on the bank of yet another river —
you, panoplied, the catch in your arms —
as ever, smiling.
Put that heavy joy down a moment, if you will.
Then shape your mouth as if for a kiss;
only, a trifle wider, so I can insert the hook.
Give me a minute or so to walk back to the house
— that way we've more line to play with —
then begin, any time at your convenience.
Nearer home, I trust you won't mind
my son snapping the times you're airborne?
And when you're tired, have fought the good fight
and come to me, that's half way to heaven
for the photo finish, as it were.
Your breath will be quite orgasmic, so many little deaths.
After that, should you look at me tenderly enough, I can
with one slight adjustment sit you on my right hand;
unless your creed would have you relish
a fishier deity, one of your own kind?
Or would you rather I unhook you like a lover a bra;
put you back where my skill found you,
holding you the right way for re-entry so
you're not bruised? So that sometime, soon,
we can have some more sport?

VEGETARIAN'S VERTIGO

They have kidnapped the girl from the cheese counter,
the meat-eating maenads from over the aisle;
they are shaving her legs with whiny razors,
plucking her head like a billiard ball.

Somewhere they have her, my dairymaid darling,
gutting her quiet as fishwives cod;
the carnivorous oafs, the file-toothy cannibals
for whom Gorgonzola is not a god.

Mommas in Stetsons are mumbling her nipples,
gibbering grandmas dividing her waist;
her eyes are a gulping dowager's oysters,
her lips escargots on charwomen's toast.

That exquisite rump's green-gruesome with parsley,
those ears on sticks in the cocktails (prawn);
and gatecrashers picking, playing her bones
like scales on a mouth organ, tuppence a tune.

O my heart's slapped wide on a windy clothesline,
my heart's beat daft as a dusty rug;
I'm lost and lone in what's coming over —
a snail in a sandstorm, a bug in a fug.

O I won't sleep tonight for the grinding of jaws,
and if I stop by tomorrow to publish my gall
what's the betting some bleached, deodorised doll
won't force-feed me processed — glazed wrapper and all?

WHEN I'M SEVENTEEN

When I'm seventeen I'm going to grab me a banger:
all dent, buckle, and clattery tin;
knocked out windows, shatter-proof shock absorbers,
tyres like ship's fenders fore and aft.
I'll get her up like an earthquake in a paintshop
(except for NEXT STOP HELL and DAVE AND WANDA – in white)
and shove in a fantastic supercharger
nicked from a spare set of aero engine plans.
And I'll enter that smasher for every event
on every track under the roaring sun.
They'll be hoarse bawling my number on the mike
as I rev fit to murder down the straight –
dance the pedals, flip the wheel,
clip the tails of the leaders slewing on the bend.
Oh I'll squeeze 'em out and smoke 'em out
and if they bash me off I'll slash screaming back
and if I come off the banking daft side up
I'll be out sharp and hungry as a weasel,
sticking my helmet on a post, sniffing oil and dust
till they tractor me off and throw me a spanner
to tighten her up and start again.
And I'll blare past the chequered flag
tall as a ship's siren, loop the pack
then sit on top with the Banger Queen –
doing my Lap Of Honour, waving to the crowd.
And Wanda will come through the blue smoke
in her green top and hair tied back.
And when I sleep that night the bed will be spinning,
cutting corners on two wheels.

AND WHY NOT?

NIGHT PEOPLE

Some back to back, staring at bitten thumbs.
Some passing blood, in agony columns.

Some cuddled up to God or Teddy.
Some lost for someone ordinary.

Some in Alhambras of spouting wands.
Some washing hot, inexhaustible hands.

Some handcuffed by loyalty, a key in a bible.
Some with God knows what certainties, tribal.

Some given peace, a conqueror's dreams.
Some nothing, hung from beams.

Some stroking dirty covers, loins of books.
Some sleepless, on adulterous tenterhooks.

Some strident, bawling stark endearments.
Some stealthy, scouting for honours in the Cents.

Some with the stuff on them, sniffing raids.
Some sweat-boxed, pleading syphilis, Aids.

Some raving at aliens, banging doors.
Some kind, taking in young whores.

Present, correct, established faces.
Nachtmusik. Textbook cases.

BALLAD OF THE AXE

O why am I sleeping with you, Gran,
not at home with Rags my teddy?
It's your Mum's turn for Rags tonight —
though I doubt she's ready.

O what will our Dad be doing now,
night shift at the mill?
Your Dad's had a friendly phone call —
and he's back to check the till.

Why has it gone so black, Gran;
not one teeny star?
They call it an eclipse, love —
the moon's got stuck in a cellar.

Gran, I dreamt she came to tell me
not to play with that knife.
Perhaps what she's wanting to say is
some things just aren't safe.

O who has taken the axe from the shed,
so keen it cuts like grass?
Your Dad has taken the axe from the shed,
to show it his favourite lass.

O who has taken the axe from the shed,
so bright it shines like silver?
Your Dad has taken the axe from the shed,
to give it to his favourite brother.

He's given him one and he's given him two
then one that kicks like a ton;
he's given him four and he's given him five
and his head's still hanging on.

He's given her six and he's given her seven —
her ribs have come apart;
he's given her eight, he's given her nine,
and the walls can see her heart.

O what's become of Uncle Ed
we used to play with in the park?
They've found him in the little wood,
mostly in a sack.

O what's become of Mum, Gran,
that used to dance light as a feather?
They've taken her down to the station,
to help piece things together.
Like a jigsaw, Gran? Like a jigsaw, love.
But what if they've lost some bits?
They go to a man called a Coroner,
who makes up what doesn't fit.

Why is it still so black, Gran;
why doesn't the moon come up?
Love, I think this is one night
she's had enough to sup.

O what's become of Dad, Gran?
He'll be somewhere changing his jacket
then down for a midnight swim in the lake
with a lump of lead in his pocket.

O when can I go to school, Gran —
there's a book I want to borrow.
You can go to school with the world, love —
when you wake up tomorrow.

THE ASSIGNMENT

I found the letter on my blanket,
by the last waterhole.
Go, find a house, post it —
that was what they said.

Before nightfall, its vulture shadows,
post it, was what they said —
before they smashed the compass, kicked out the fire,
that was what they said.

Through scorpion cacti, rattler's rocks,
over sands tossed with camel skulls,
the sun prodding me like a gun
I marched to early afternoon

and in the middle of the plain found it:
two storeys, the bottom curtainless,
the top (entered by a fire escape)
shuttered, clammed up like a fist.

'Hello' I bawled. 'Anyone at home?'
A gnawed bone gaped from the fence;
with a burnt hole where the nipple pokes
a child's vest hung on a line.

There was a half-finished path of sorts,
in its cement the print of a child's shoe;
and by the gate a tiny phial of perfume —
unstoppered, sunlicked dry.

Boots battering the iron steps
I went up, banged on the door.
'Anyone at home? Hello. Hello . . .'
and my voice, dying of itself.

The letter box had a steel flap,
tough, tight as lockjaw.
I pried it open like a cat's mouth,
shoved the sweaty letter halfway in.

Silence. Nothing. Only
a clock ticking, a woman's scent.
Then suddenly, a lizard's scamper —
something that tiptoed, naked, small.

Silence, tracking me down the path.
The tinkle of a phial, broken.
Something slammed like a pistol shot.
Something giggling into a fist of hair.

'You smell of women' they said.
'What's that on your boot?'
'Cement' I said. 'What's that in your hand?'
'The answer to a letter' I said.

A LOOK AT THE 'D' WORD

Gran in that shroud-and-shit-coloured ward
snatching her wash-thin blanket to her,
jerking away from touch, breath almost snarling
into its last impregnable sleep;

Ruth 'going home to fight'.
Three days later a felled tree,
beside it someone with locked hands
trying to master a sobbing mouth;

Bill: shredded lungs
fish-opening his maw for another squirt,
his lame wife dragging the floor to the door knob,
heaving herself up to lend a neighbour a quarter of tea...

between 'c' for creation and 'e' for earth — that word.
Eventually it comes to us to accept it.
All we can do is fuck it up with love.
Something cheap, universal. A quarter of tea.

BIRTHDAY GREETINGS TO MYSELF AT SEVENTY-FOUR

Three score and ten plus. Every second nicked
above the biblical whack you pay for, Jack.
No one gets owt for nowt, chum.
Up goes the carpet, you're on your bum.

Time out massaging a nutty cut,
poncing up roses or just sieving shit —
it's there on that black incorrigible slate
above the bar. And no rebate.

Loan sharks peddling hallucinogens,
vulpine uncles, twitchy hit men,
they'll be along for iced coffee this afternoon
with guess who as the patsy, the gone goon.

The Muse will doubtless show up as well
with a Dantesque snap or two of hell;
Shylock — after his bloody pound —
and his mate the sexton, looking for common ground.

Nota bene, Senex — you're off the rota;
you've had your quota, your fireproof motor.
Worms, warlocks, they're tossing for keeps;
the crabs are in there, and the scavenger jeeps.

You're in it way above your hoary head,
in Queer Street, Fear Street, the running red:
one for the drop, a sack of crap
to be disposed of — fast — by the bent cop.

Somewhere that schlock you write's in hock,
limbo friendly, old cock.
Somewhere its Redeemer liveth, maybe?
Likelier, toes up in a disused lay-by.

You were shunted in, you'll be shunted out;
one for the road, one more for the rout.
Starter's Orders due. On your mark, Surplus.
Last man to kiss the wreath's a sourpuss.

FLESH

Our bodies know better than we do
when it's time to quit;
no longer put up with this havering
of drivel-heads, these creeping zeros.

They have enough of the grainy farmer in them
to probe a sky, predict
tomorrow's cloud-mess — how needful it is
to wrap up against it.

Equally to know that old duds
are nothing against the inward drizzle,
the clamp of cold that honeycombs the bone,
strangulates what's left of brain.

They go on because other bodies like it,
to see a peep of life yet in cooling embers,
a tinge of blood still about.
But themselves, they don't want it.

And their dreams walk an open field,
praying for lightning's godly act —
a last favour, that will flash them out,
earth them forever, no more fear or fuss.

SATIRIST

To begin with a sheet, unwritten drama
and the dead face looking out of the page,
its eyes peristalsis in a crow's belly.

To go on with words, ants oblivious of what they tread on,
crossing the skull of space
with a coded implant, a set sting.

To end with substance, through other eyes;
in a lamb's wool coat, a flak jacket,
engage, scarify, persuade.

BEDSIDE MANNERS

My wife's always blasting on about inhibition —
why drystick to the missionary position?
I say praise the Lord and control the ammunition,
she pukes at that — where's my erudition,
and come to that, my shagmasterly ambition?
She wants to shake it up with a bit of sedition,
savour the subtle joys of carnal collision
swung from a chandelier.., which stark illumination
I'll do without (without hesitation);
or sway astride me with Ben Hur-like precision,
or be taken palindromic for the odd session.
She bets me a stallion's tassel Lilian Gish'n
Valentino didn't simplify their passion,
not to mention Caravaggio, Goya and Titian;
tells me my Kraft's ebbing, that De Sade was a magician
to be venerated, part of the human condition;
that variety would spice up my glands and my dentition,
that I should clean my plug, check over my ignition.
I say it's all too much for my hernia's reputation,
that my screwed testes could suffer elision,
nor has my bishop Mary Whitehouse's permission.
If it's really a case of sensory deprivation
why not the schoolgirl stand by, masturbation;
or if the drag's the hetero sapiens situation
— same folks, same wayside station —
rake the dog's home for a touch of genuine Alsatian?
That's flashpoint. Suddenly the air's gentian
with practised fury, sprawls, shouts for attention:
a raving local tourney of attrition
sparked with sly fibs and thunderous accusation,
banged bedheads, pillow-flagellation —
at whose limp fagend (if neighbourly intervention
hasn't shown its appetite for this week's edition
by rousing the fuzz to summary eviction)
we doze off, still no glint of a decision —
she to a disco of unspeakable relations
— python navvies, pneumatic drill vibrations —
me to dream of some calmer sutra . . .
like — heavenly norm — the missionary position.

BLUE FILMS

These aficionados so dramatically at it —
angling their carrots, their bossy boobs,
twiddling frantic nipples, wiping tongue on tongue —
these topsy-turvy bareback braves
quirting the bedsprings, scalping each other's moans —
from climax to head-squirmed suffocating climax
where do they live, apart from this?

Why do they never show the rest of it —
post-triumphant coasting its quiet level
with surrendered skis, no more plying to impress?
Never the mindful details that make love —
shifting the weight to propped elbows,
sorting the duvet so that feet aren't cold,
doodling filigree edges, squeezing a sleepy thigh,
giving the dovetailed miracle its ark?

EARLY, LATE

Hopscotch through the maze of boughs
long-tailed tits jink and flicker,
calling to each other like girls on an outing,
the flirty streamers of their tails preened for fiesta.

Provocative, slender, their voices wink
incessant as knitting needles. I think
of old women purling away in upstairs windows,
watching youth's blind-flying zest —

old women, who have the pattern by heart.

CENOTAPH

The village instance, green sandstone,
with its rosette-pronged cross,
scuffed dates, clannish names
— you never see hands about it
yet somehow things arrive:
hoops of poppies bowl in from somewhere,
suddenly the plinth's alive
with chrysanths and dahlias, quiverfuls
flaring from conscripted off-the-shelf pots.

Such relentless care. You'd have thought
the generation behind it
would have died out by now.
So why should descendants keep it up?
Unless it's habit, a touchstone feeling
that somehow it's all right, and if
one reneges on its observance, guilt will glare?

And winds slice in from the east, leaving
jarred, splintered blooms on the cobbles,
tongues of drying water . . .
'our Ted' and 'our Ben' . . .
who will be now, may one ask, where?

Upwards, some would say,
pointing with love, that tenacious idiocy,
to the hanging basket of stars.

THAT THING

It should be neat, funny: a spoof thriller
laid lightly down at the end.

It should be quick, kind: a child falling
asleep on its father's shoulders.

As it is, no one wants it
— not the flower at her scented zenith

nor the pontiff in his holy litter —
only the cenotaph its white invention

whose name-dropping alibi
needs, invites it.

RIVER BANK

Someone in that high, ample house
is stroking the petals of a piano —
Schubert, cantabile, floats from an open window.

The limes have nodded into leaf.
A girl tickles the sleepy head
in her lap with a plume of grass.

And on the bike-leant bridge a boy
nipping across to see
the dandelion head he dropped

glow out on the other side.

UNCOLLECTED POEMS

DUSK

I am following a shrinking man

I am following a shuffling man
who is trying to plough with his toes

I am following a heartless man

I am following a man with a quiver of pain
whose arrows ricochet

I am following a man whose cord whips me
whom I am bound to follow

I am following a man who remembers me
only in snatches

I am following a man whose last and first eucharist
is potassium permanganate and toast

I am following a man who does not know
I am behind him

they tell me I must catch him
I do not want to

I am following a shivering man with an earn of sand
on his shoulder

I am following a man with a key sewn into a glove
he has lost

I do not have time not to follow him

I am following a man with a telegram of hope
he will never get

I am following a man

WORLD WAR TWO CALENDAR

Shakespeare Day

When we heard on the barrack room radio
the Nazis were into Holland
what Sam came up with was:
"Will you toss me off, Red?"

Then there was that Normandy peasant, told
how shrapnel had missed me
just by a swished foot —
who said 'Parfait!"

Sergeant Will, that symphonic microphone,
might have put it differently, in blank verse,
but picked this much up from history —
the best lines come with bit parts,

Sherlock Holmes Day

Why was the old lady sitting in the lorry?
The child running backwards through the snow?
What was the link between the sapper
his dead mate's paybook
and the canary in the shelled house?
Why was the nun's birthmark a swastika?
Who was the hook-nosed stranger that didn't stay?
What was the General doing, betting on advances?
How did the last letter get sent first?
Why was the war still on?

Good Friday

Most I remember of that road to Dunkirk
is passing two lads in the middle of a field.
sandbag-coracled behind a Vickers that looked
as if remaindered from the '14 -'18 war,

No one else for kilometres —
facing back, that was.
They would save maybe ten minutes,
a small boatload.

Saint Patrick's Day

The RC Padre.
that Irish cavalier
who'd twinkled
his flute on the plane
and jumped
with a rose in his helmet —
when the first casualties came in
went to sleep.

Though he wouldn't have offered
a dead man a fag
when he got wounded
one had sympathy:
it was only Christian.

V E Day

A hospital on the Baltic coast.
its courtyard boasting an Aryan ikon
— strong, joyful buttocks,
a cloned eagle at its plinthed feet —

waving the tambourine of a laurel wreath
towards a New Order, sieg-heiling a future
where corridors of born again heroes
masterwalked miles of never-to-be-needed beds . . .

the same corridors now thick with the stench of shit
that watch torpid remnants lost for drugs
stroke bony brows, stiffen what's left of limbs
with paper bandages

while downtown the champions — battalion lads —
wrestle with rusty peace and each other —
bellow, cackle, hiccup,
bang off tracer at absent stars

and alone in the billet you're back twenty years,
remembering that child given his first sparkler;
running fiery harmless rings
round a November garden.

OLD THOUGHTS WALKING ON A FINE NIGHT

I am no longer at risk
from moth-woven dusk
or the piercing absolute of a star.

This blood's too old
to wear adventure
or further arterial scarring.

Time to vacate it seems;
leave hearth-embers
for the stench of dearth —

bequeath
the scant brain
a senseless present

allow the failing heart
its alibi
in death

THE LEGACY

Trunks thundering up from beechfall;
midway, the quarry in the clearing,
moss-matched boulders like half-hewn torsos —
we loved it, that fellside wood.

Near the summit, rivulets dribbled
into an old tank roofed with settled leaves;
if sunbeams were happening and you parted those leaves
you might see a newt free-falling

and higher, on the tableland of its top,
a stone pond patrolled by dragonflies
— skimming, jabbing, hovering
above their short shadows.

We had a favourite rock, twin-slabbed,
sloped like an eight foot granite lectern —
there we'd stretch, into the cloud-tossed sky...
the breeze bubbling my shirt, wisping your hair,
tender as if it were swabbing a pair of babes.

How could we guess, then, that wind would turn,
a glacial past come to overtake us —
operating its random, helpless law
strike one into effigy?

TENSES

Somewhere, will be that town of people
where everyone is doing something else;
busy ungetting it together,
their eyes anywhere but straight.

Bedlam. Not even quiet enough
to realise it's come to that.

Here in this village graveyard meanwhile
there's a swish of lilac to lift remembered nostrils;
and headstones in togas of grass
chiming companionably to tombs.

The past has done its time,
is laid back about it.

Between, I shut the gate,
prod listless shanks towards a supposed future.
A jogger steaming by sends up my heartbeat,
leaves me an echo, limping.

A LATE GIFT

Windy drizzle of leaves falling . . .
the lawn a spilt card table.
Yet, one rose. Proustian survivor,
it has scent for us; backdated summer
whets our pinched nostrils.
And we inhale, hail a transplanted past;
a lost season spruce as a croupier flashing
welcome, unwrapping a fresh deck.

TIME SHARE

When the curly-stemmed cyclamen
blushed open on the lid
of that old Singer you never use

unsheathing the bendy rapiers of their tongues
Red Admirals
targeted our buddleia

when you came down from the orchard that day
your hands blueshadowy
with ripe damsons

the yaffle laughed and tattooed the very trunk
we'd tipped as
his likeliest

when the baby bat flew out of afternoon tiles
so close there wasn't a whisper of light
between them

for all such times of four-eyed wonder
I, too haphazard ever
to bless you with anything on its approved date

send it now
— in a few I hope concise words —
a year's Valentine.

BENCH-MARKS

Nothing new happens, says the old man on the bench.
There's only the old, that don't.
If you can still smell you'll catch the stench.

Not enough money, too much wrench.
Even if it still would like to, it won't.
Nothing new happens, says the old man on the bench.

We're up to our crutches in a wet trench.
We'd cry. But — more water? We can't.
If you can still smell you'll catch the stench.

The knives are out; stropped, raring to flench.
If it was once well now it ain't.
Nothing new happens, says the old man on the bench.

Today nothing. Tomorrow maybe the crunch?
There were those before us. Ubi sunt?
If you can still smell you'll catch the stench.

And then, that lordly shepherd. Grass for lunch.
Clover to come, if you've the urge to repent.
Nothing new happens, says the old man on the bench.
If you can still smell you'll catch the stench.

AFTER RAIN

The beck wallops by
like a fat farm wench
in floppy slippers.

I follow my love
into July grass.
It swoons in her wake,
every blade
unearthing raindrops.

Fresh as Christmas fivepences
in a child's quicksilver dream
they rush to meet me.

HERO

I salute what's done and who did it:
a poetic torso grandly knit
as anything Lysippus cast
for Grecian light to marvel at

but today, in the fickle body with him,
pity loses me, all I see, hear
is a burping diabetic daring his flabby gut
to accept a smidgin of torte,
an old man in his bladder-stung small hours
wrenching out of sleep's ragged eiderdown
to piss once more, piss the night away
with tiny compelled voidings

he who in days of triumph
would drink till dawn cracked the sky open
arguing the tilt of a sentence,
the plot of a line

one of a matchless archipelago of makars
crumbling it seems almost
competitively now

some of whom cannot gather enough
to even remember a time when
their pasts spoke to each other.

I think of them, of him, only hope
my love and thanks reach him sufficiently
to bless what's left, what days remain . . .

knowing I want too much, of course.

SNOW FOLK

Today's different We rise to fluffy trees,
branches penstroked in —

and a garden beyond itself.
Seat felted, greenhouse lagged.

Some cloud's been breaking extra bread,
whitening sills with crumbs.

Touting for browner fare a robin arrives
on tiny skis

then — fence-sneaked — next door's setter;
leaving the lawn slotted with lollopy trespass.

Soon no doubt we'll see its owner's kids
set freezing, stubborn hands to sculpting him —

his flatcapped, carrot-schnozzled bonce
(with that forked twig of a mouth)

will stare across at our anaemic front
and lord it for a couple of days

until a touch of sun undoes his bluff,
mortified he either cries himself elsewhere

or slumps — presumably strangled
by that red, dropped noose of a scarf.

FATHER WILLIAM IS SOMEWHAT EXERCISED

Oh doctor doctor what's this trickling down my leg?
I feel like a baby stood up in the bath.
Is it the moment of baptismal truth?
More like your prostate, Willie, becoming a touch uncouth.

Oh doctor doctor I have this heart-twinge.
Can it be Cupid's dart? Am I the bull's eye cert,
just another would-be horny old fart
set up as sport-fodder for Mom the dove-eyed tart?

Oh doctor doctor are these blotches on my hands
stigmata? Is it my week as Recycled Orderly Martyr?
Or will falsetto lead in the Castrati's Cantata
suit me better (and give the punters at least a dram of laughter)?

Oh doctor doctor is this the Om Mantra
or the Great Hive Of Heaven buzzing up my ear?
What's that you're saying? From what I hear
merely wax or tinnitus my God-bothered old dear.

Oh doctor doctor my zapper won't zoom.
What price a lightning tup-graft to make it a good ole boy?
Don't say it's sit down and die, nevermore poke that sly
tulip-flange up from a naughty fly?

Oh doctor doctor one minute I've lost my pulse
the next it's roaring away like a typewriter on fire.
When did the stress start? Was it so dire,
the day my teararse gerbils dropped in on the Ladies Choir?

Oh doctor daddy I went out of my body last night —
who d'you think I saw at the end of the tunnel?
Sylvia P, in her floral nightie. And — in see-through sandals —
who else but Stearnsie, chairing the Admissions Panel.

Oh doctor doctor I have this dream —
of a turbaned T-shirt splashed RIM GIPA:
come to mow the lawn, with one of those super-duper
Schwarzenegger-type slashers so dear to loony snoopers.

Oh Willie Willie you desperate old curio
count your balmy blessings not your unlucky dips.
D'you think J.C's so stuck for folk he wants you up top?
Go back to your Audenary slippers, those post-prandial coach trips.

You've time to get born again, paddle to evensong,
sprout a new dong — you've got away with it so long!

AS IF IT MATTERED

The fact of the matter is – matter.
No matter how we natter on
matter was there before matter
and ever shall be muck without end –
sticking to its agenda
braced to put us through the blender.

Who came up with matter's another matter –
we know it wasn't the anthropomorphic squatter
(in any case HE's persona non grata
doesn't merit a logical vote)
nor for that matter do those hunting and hawking
cosmologists who blatter on crying
'the question's irrelevant, can't matter'.

Meanwhile, breasting such spindrift chatter,
mad as a million hatters,
Matter, Canute and King, goes on mattering;
splitting, shattering into creative tatters,
triggering, sparking off
audible edible incredible new data
more than enough for anyone's post-atomic platter

and what it does with us and we with it
clatter or splatter neither one of us knows
only if one goes down t'other's with it
lickety-split tough shit
and of the two it's homo sapiens that flops,
sick on the sidewalk, with an aching crop,
while Old Man Matter – maybe a smidgin fatter –
still keeps rolling along . . .
at least until the time he's begat a-
nother planet to flatten or flatter,
another can of wormy hominoids to scatter . . .

unless it's us again, into a barmier karma,
recycled, retyred, reincarnated,
listening crypt-wrapped as John Brown Matter
goes mouldering, marching on . . .

on song for Nirvana or the next con
muck without end alleluia amen.

THE GENETICS OF SNOW

I do not understand it —

how anyone taking the time
to iron a shirt,
spread immaculate napery

should sponsor bazookas of wind
that batter cars
into bloated shrouds;

how the wizard of apples,
statues, white laughter
can sit siameasy with him who scatters
wafers of a host fundamentalist
as cluster bombs;

how the surgeon operating with light
in the stainless kingdom of trust
is also that camp guard bingeing on death
like a diabetic with a Christmas cake.

I do not understand it.

Nor, it seems, anything else.

MIGRANT

for Gerda Mayer

My daughter has gone away
to find someone in the city.
This is the first Spring
we have not looked for nests.